Missi Jenkins

HOW TO
STUDY
THE BIBLE
AND
ENJOY IT

Skip Heitzig

D1042729

CONNECTION COMMUNICATIONS
4001 OSUNA ROAD NORTHEAST • ALBUQUERQUE , NEW MEXICO 87111 USA

How To Study the Bible and Enjoy It
by Skip Heitzig

ISBN1-886324-00-X

Published by CONNECTION PUBLISHING
Cover design by Stephen T. Eames
Printed in the USA

Dedication

This volume is affectionately dedicated to
Chuck Smith
my mentor and friend who gave me a
love for the Word of God.
His unselfish ministry and unswerving commitment
to teaching God's truths
have been a continual source of inspiration
to me through the years.

And to the wonderful people
that make up the flock of
Calvary of Albuquerque,
a church filled with people who love to
read the Word,
hear the Word,
study the Word,
and obey the Word.
It has been sheer delight
to stand week after week
and teach the Bible
to such eager and hungry hearts.

Table of Contents

Getting Prepared, Getting Excited

The Scriptures were not given to increase our knowledge but to change our lives. —D.L. Moody

Of the many radical changes that accompany spiritual conversion, perhaps none is more significant than a shift in attitude toward the Bible. Before salvation, the Bible is generally viewed as a historical book written in antiquated language, containing some noble principles. What a surprise, when our spiritual eyes are opened, to find that the Bible is the Word of God; an inexhaustible treasure of truth and wisdom! Even better, there can be real *enjoyment* in Bible study. Though this joy of discovery is readily available to all sincere seekers, it is not automatic. While the Bible's message is basically simple, thorough and thoughtful study is by no means easy. I've written this book to serve as a prod, something to whet the appetite for the proper approach to consistent study of the Bible.

Every week Christians all over this country carry their Bibles to church. Of course, we live in a country where this is still legal. There are countries where you aren't allowed to own one. Most American households have a Bible but, unfortunately, few really understand how to study it and apply the principles found within. For too many, the Bible is a confusing combination of stuffy old stories, ancient history, and irrelevant rules.

After I became a Christian, I went back to the church in which I was raised. Although it was considered a Christian denomination, Bible reading was never emphasized. I entered the front door of the church, Bible in hand, and wound my way through the foyer. People looked at me as though I was an extra-terrestrial being. "Why are you bringing in one of *those things?*" someone asked. I thought, "What am I supposed to carry? A coloring book?"

Certainly, the Bible is the book for the church. It is our Magna Carta, our Declaration of Independence. It is our owner's manual and our road map to life. I agree with George Mueller, founder of the Bristol Orphanage in London, during the last century. He said this about God's word:

The vigor of our spiritual life will be in exact proportion to the place held by the Bible in our life and thoughts. I solemnly state this from the experience of 54 years. The first 3 years after conversion I neglected the word of God. Since I began to search it diligently the blessing has been wonderful. Great has been the blessing from consecutive, diligent, daily study. I look upon it as a lost day when I have not had a good time over the Word of God.

But we need to *understand* what the Bible says to us or else it will be of no value to us. "What do the words of all those prophets, poets, and pundits have to do with me and my life today? It all seems so—*distant.*" That's how lots of people feel about the Bible.

Let's suppose a friend sent you a letter. You open it with eager anticipation only to frown as you see a confusing message, "Uzza wuzza jazza wazza! Surfuss murfuss calorex flex." You think, "Humm, what could this mean? A joke perhaps? Maybe this is a secret code or another language he has learned." To you, it's nothing but gibberish. Unless someone interprets it for you, you are at a loss.

Many people look at the Bible the same way. They suppose it's a cryptic code that needs to be broken and deciphered. Some think they need an expert to explain the truths in it; they feel they must go away to school or take a course to *really* understand its message. Hogwash! It certainly *is* a book from God, and being divine in origin, it is unique from all other books. Yet God has taken our frailties into consideration and has given us His Word in such a way that our souls can be nourished by it.

In these chapters, I will explain some very basic tools that will help any believer feel at home just about anywhere in the Bible. You don't have to be afraid of any portion of the Scripture. After all, the Holy Spirit is the real author. He knew what He was doing as He orchestrated its composition and preservation.

When British poet and statesman, Sir Walter Scott, was on his death bed, he summoned his assistant and said, "Bring me the book." His assistant indulged Scott's wishes but then challenged him by asking, "Sir Scott, you have so many volumes in your library. Which book shall I bring you?" Scott's retort was poignant. "Bring me the *book*, the Bible—the only book for a dying man." Sir Walter Scott was correct. But the Bible is not only the book for dying men. It is the book for the living, as well.

It's All Greek To Me!

One of the things people may not realize is that the New Testament was written in sort of a "market-place" Greek. In this simple style, the "average man on the street" could understand it. There were basically two types of ancient Greek: a classical, refined style that was unique to scholars, and a simpler style known as *Koine*, or common Greek. It was the style of the Greek-speaking world from the time of Alexander the Great until about A.D. 500. Don't get me wrong, I'm not saying that every portion of the Bible is simple; certainly there are hard and controversial parts. As Paul put it, we only "know in part," but someday we'll see the full picture of truth. Until then, I am content to be "on hold" about some of these things.

I like the way one minister responded when he was challenged about the Bible. He was traveling by train, enjoying his lunch of New England codfish—the kind that has bones in every bite. An agnostic was sitting across from him and noticed the minister's Bible. "You believe in that book?" asked the skeptic.

"Yes, every word of it," replied the minister.

Arrogantly, the agnostic pressed on, "Really? Do you understand it all?"

With a smile, the pastor answered, "Of course not. The Bible is not without its difficulties."

Thinking he was backing the clergyman into a theological corner, the agnostic asked, "Then what do you do about all those difficulties in the Bible?"

The man of God skillfully held his own and explained, "Look, it's like this fish I'm eating. I just eat the fish. I leave the bones for some other fool to choke on!"

So even though there are some difficult bumps in the Bible road, let's be content to study the Scripture in faith and leave the rest to God. Chuck Smith put it this way, "Never give up what you *do* know for sure for what you *don't* know for sure." Awesome advice. Hold on to what you know for certain—those things God reveals to you in His Word. Create a little mental file and entitle it, "Waiting for Further Information." As you study, you will grow, and the file will grow as well.

Does God Use Human Teachers?

Since the Holy Spirit dwelling inside us puts all believers on an even playing field, the question arises, *do* we need human teachers? I'll let the Apostle Paul answer that one:

> *And He Himself gave some to be apostles, some prophets, some evangelists, and some pastors and teachers, for the equipping of the saints for the work of ministry, for the edifying of the body of Christ.* (Eph. 4:11-12)

This is how it works: God gives teachers, pastors, and others to help the church understand the meaning of Scripture. These gifted people are used by God to help equip God's people for works of service. There's nothing wrong with being taught by those whom God has gifted to do so.

Once a highly schooled pastor went to preach at a quaint little country church. A frowning man approached him after the service and said, "Brother, God kin git along without all your learnin'."

The preacher's reply was classic. He said, "Yes sir, God can. And He can also get along without your ignorance."

Being taught by others is not the only way we learn. The Holy Spirit resides in every believer to direct us into the truth of God. When Jesus was still on earth, He promised His followers that the Holy Spirit would teach them all things and guide them into all truth. Because the Holy Spirit is the real author of Scripture, He is the best Bible teacher. Every time Christians open the Bible, they can rely on the Holy Spirit to illuminate the text.

Sometimes as Christians, we can become conditioned to being spoon-fed the Scripture. After all, it's great to sit and listen to a well-versed Bible teacher and just soak it in. The teacher does all the work and we do all the sitting and soaking, right? Actually, the most rewarding truths are those that are self-discovered, as the Holy Spirit sheds light on the Scriptures. When we discover truth from our own study, our personal convictions are much deeper and more permanent than if those truths had been told to us.

Perhaps you've had the same experience I've had. You've read a Scripture several times, then you read it again, and this time a light goes on. It's as if the fog has rolled away and it's clearer than ever before. Now, when you refer to that Scripture, you've got real insight. What happened? The Holy Spirit simply did what Jesus promised He would do—He led you into all truth. I think the perfect balance of the teachings of human teachers and the Holy Spirit was found by the Bereans, a group of Christians Paul met on his travels. He was impressed that they were unique and diligent students of the Bible:

These were more fair-minded than those in Thessalonica, in that they received the word with all readiness, and searched the Scriptures daily to find out whether these things were so. (Acts 17:11)

Notice the balance between receiving truth and searching it out. We should receive the truth from teachers, preachers, and mature Christians God puts in our lives, but we should not stop there. The Bereans even scrutinized Paul's teaching in the light of Scripture, and Paul commended their actions. So listen readily to your pastor, but always check it out to see if his words align with God's. As we become students of the Scripture, not just being fed a little bottle every week, we will see an acceleration in our spiritual growth. We will experience the incomparable ministry of the Holy Spirit as He speaks to us personally.

Actually, one of healthiest habits you can develop is to read regularly through the entire Bible. Now before you gulp and dismiss the idea as too difficult, let's put it in perspective. It's not as formidable a task as you might think. At a very moderate rate, the entire Bible can be read in about 70 hours. That works out to about 52 hours for the Old Testament and 18 hours for the New Testament. Even the longest portion of the Old Testament, like the Psalms, takes only 4 and a half hours to read, while the Gospel of Luke would occupy less than 3 hours. Not as time-consuming as you'd think, is it? Compare that with the time you spend on other activities. For most of us, for instance, making a living consumes at least 40 hours a week. Week in and week out, that's about 2,000 hours annually. Each year we sleep almost 3,000 hours. Add another 550 hours per year for eating (give or take a few), and about 1,500 hours per year for watching television. Perspective is everything!

2

Having the Right Tools

I have covenanted with my Lord that He should not send me visions or dreams or even angels. I am content with this gift of the Scriptures, which teaches and supplies all that is necessary, both for this life and that which is to come.

—Martin Luther

The right tools are essential in any project. Ask anyone who's tried to do a job without them. When an artist sets out to express himself on canvas, he first makes sure his palette, paints, and brushes are at hand. A carpenter knows he must be equipped with his hammer, saw, plane, and nails before setting out to frame that house. A photographer loads his camera with film before trying to capture his subject through the lens. In the same manner, we need the right tools to capture God's truth in our hearts.

Let's start with the basics: the first and best tool for Bible study is the Bible. I know that might sound a bit simplistic and obvious, but you would be surprised at how many people study about the Bible rather than study the *Bible itself.* Some amass a great library of volumes, thinking these books are necessary to adequately understand the Bible. While many of these books are helpful and beneficial, the best study tool for the Bible is still the Bible. All others are important but secondary.

The next important tool is a simple notebook to record what God reveals to you personally as you read. Even the great evangelist Dwight L. Moody made it a habit of carrying a notebook to record the truths God imparted to him as he read the Bible or listened to sermons. As you make it your daily practice to read, study, and learn from God in His Word, you'll discover the joy of God *personally revealing* His will for your life.

J. Wilbur Chapman wrote the following guidelines for Bible study:

Study it through. *Start each day by mastering a verse from its pages.*

Pray it in. *Meditate on the verse or passage until it becomes part of your being.*

Put it down. *Record in your notebook or Bible the thoughts God gives you.*

Work it out. *Live the truth you get in the morning through each hour of the day.*

The first step is to find a Bible that you can consistently read and study. It should be accurate, easy to read, and one you can carry wherever you go. Fortunately, there are a lot of styles and versions to choose from.

Unfortunately, that makes the choice more difficult. Today, asking which is the best Bible to buy may thrust you into the midst of a debate you didn't know existed.

When Purchasing a Bible

Maybe you've had the experience of walking into a Christian bookstore to buy a Bible and finding it to be a jungle of versions, study systems, and binding colors. What begins as a simple shopping trip can result in being overwhelmed with the range of choices. What version should you get—New International Version? New American Standard? New King James? Should you get the Red Letter Edition? And what about references—do you want center or side column reference? Bonded or natural leather? Burgundy, black, navy, or mauve? To say we are blessed in this country, and in our day and age, with a variety of Bible translations would be an understatement.

You may not have heard of the "Valley Version." Targeted for the Southern California audience, Jesus says, "For sure, for sure, I say unto you, dude!" Then there's the *Punk Rock Study Bible*. Rather than Red Letter, the words of Jesus are in glow-in-the-dark orange. Of course, these don't really exist, but there are many choices to make when buying your own Bible.

When making your selection, a Bible with a center or side column reference is good. This will enable you to look up verses of Scripture which relate to the ones you are currently reading, giving you a balanced perspective of the teachings of the Bible as a whole. A wide-margin-ed Bible allows you to write your own comments and observations next to the Bible text so your notes are always there. Study Bibles are widely available and very popular. *Scofield Reference Bible*, the *Ryrie Study Bible*, the *Thompson Chain Reference Study Bible*, the *NIV Study Bible*, and the *Life Application Bible* are a few of the excellent selections which can be found in most Christian bookstores. Be aware that some study Bibles have the notes and interpretation of difficult passages already written out at the bottom of the page. While this can be a handy aid, there is a danger of becoming lazy and automatically looking at the printed notes rather than meditating on the passage yourself. Remember, those notes are not the inspired Word of God; they are commentaries on the historical and cultural back-ground, and oftentimes, the publisher's opinions. As you read the Bible and come to difficult passages, don't automatically look to a commentary or study note. Learn to examine and question it yourself. Look up cross references to the passage. Ask God to reveal Himself to you in a unique way in that text.

A young woman once purchased a book and, after reading a few pages, laid it aside as uninteresting. Some time later, she became acquainted with the author. A tender friendship sprang up, which ripened into love and betrothal. Then the book was no longer dull. Every sentence held a charm for her heart. Love was the interpreter!

Two Basic Versions

No English-speaking generation has ever been better served with Bible versions than ours. There are two basic types of translations. One is called the "dynamic equivalent" version which sacrifices word and sentence structure for smooth reading. Their aim is the total impact of the Scripture on the believer. The translators attempted to make the message as impacting to the modern reader as it was to the ancient reader when he read it in his own vernacular. The New International Version (NIV) has served this generation well and is a good example of a dynamic equivalent version. Others have also followed this style for modern readers. J. B. Phillips' *New Testament in Modern English* is one that has become popular as well.

The second type of translation is the "word for word equivalent." This approach often sacrifices smooth English for a literal translation. It attempts to give a word for word, clause for clause, and sentence for sentence rendering of the original text. The New American Standard and The King James are two notable versions that continue in popularity. One recent addition to the family of translations is The New King James Version. The translators of this version claim to take the approach of "complete equivalence." This principle seeks to preserve all of the information in the text, while presenting it in good literary form.

Some will no doubt ask about *The Living Bible.* While proven to be helpful, be aware that it is not a translation at all, but a "transliteration" or commentary. Kenneth Taylor wanted to rewrite the Bible in a way that could be understood by his children. Unfortunately, he didn't take into consideration text, context, or sentence structure. It is a very simple commentary that could be used as a reference to bring out meaning in some cases, but it is not totally accurate. *The Amplified Bible* is another transliteration/commentary and is also a good Bible for comparison and study. However, if you are using *The Living Bible* or *The Amplified Bible* as your primary Bible, I suggest you wean yourself from it as soon as possible and move on to a solid translation.

Find a Bible you like and stick with that version as your primary Bible. You might want to get a couple of versions to bring alongside for comparison as you are doing your daily or weekly studies. You can also get a "parallel Bible" which contains 4 differing translations under one cover. I have even found a 3-volume set that contains 26 translations (Don't be too shocked—that's only a smattering of the available translations). These are all good for comparison but can be very confusing if you try to read them just for the sake of reading. For both studying and teaching, I prefer The New King James version, though I often refer to other translations to compare wording.

Other Tools

There are a few other helpful aids that can enhance your adventure in Bible study. The sky is the limit as far as what's available, so be careful and choose wisely. If you don't, you may find yourself up to your neck in unused books and unpaid bills from the Bible bookstore. The last thing anyone needs is an impressive set of theology books that wind up as an expensive doorstop! Here are a few suggestions if you want to start a library:

Concordance: A concordance is simply an alphabetized index of every word in the Bible and a listing of every passage in which it appears. It enables you to find a passage when you can only remember a word or two of it. Have you ever scratched your head and said to yourself, "Where is the verse that talks about guidance? It's gotta be somewhere in the Old Testament—but where?" That's when a concordance comes in handy. If you're able to buy additional tools, get a good concordance. You'll find it to be a good navigational tool in Bible study. Again, there are several to choose from. *Strong's Concordance* and *Young's Concordance* are known as *exhaustive* concordances because they contain a complete (exhaustive) listing of every indexed word. They are invaluable for word studies and cross-reference work. Some come equipped with short definitions of most of the Bible words, translated from the original languages. *Cruden's Concordance* is another fine option. The great Victorian preacher, Charles Spurgeon, wrote in its flyleaf, "For these ten years this has been the book at my left hand when the Word of God has been at my right." Nowadays, there is a matching concordance for every Bible version. For instance, the *NIV Bible* has the NIV Complete Concordance, and the New King James Version also has a matching concordance. Today's modern computer technology has made compiling such works much easier and faster.

Bible Dictionary: If you want to go a bit further in Bible Study, a good Bible dictionary will greatly help. As the term implies, this tool gives meanings to words, topics, and places. It is a general informational tool about the contents of the Bible. And once again, you will be faced with a variety from which to choose. Bible dictionaries summarize a word or a subject, giving historical background and additional insight. Its approach is topical and provides biblical references on your subject. Many of these works have great photographs, maps, and even small atlases so you can get the general "feel" of the particular place you are reading about. Since there are many contributors to a Bible dictionary, it will give the reader a well-rounded knowledge of many Bible subjects. Also available in most Christian book stores are Bible dictionaries that provide insights into the languages the Bible was written in: Greek, Hebrew, and Aramaic.

Commentaries: These are books written by scholars who make comments about the Bible. There are many different kinds with many different types of comments. Some comments are good and some can be, well, pretty lame. The whole purpose of a Bible commentary is to serve as an aid to interpretation and understanding. There are one-volume commentaries available, as well as two-volume sets for the Old Testament and the New Testament. You can also find commentaries with multiple volumes for those with the extra cash and interest. *The New Bible Commentary* contains concise opinions by godly authors along with additional information, making it a good tool. Other one-volume commentaries are by Ungers and Wycliffe. Since these kinds of books are popular new ones are produced and published every year, making it impossible to adequately discuss them all. If you want more than one volume, you might want to get Jameson Faucett Brown's, or Matthew Henry's commentary for a more devotional slant on Scripture. Almost all the major publishers of Christian literature provide good commentaries of the Bible. I recommend that you visit your local Christian bookstore and spend some time with a few commentaries. Pretend you're interviewing them for the job. Take the portion of Scripture you are most familiar with and compare how commentators treat the passage. Then make your choice based on your observations. Allow me to issue a small warning here. Be careful not to lean too heavily on these, lest you become dependent on them and lose your love for digging into the Bible for yourself. There's nothing like getting it firsthand. And besides, their comments are simply that—comments. They are helpful but not inspired. Make it your practice to go right to the source and skip the middleman as much as possible.

Computer Bible Programs: Whether you like it or not, it's time to face the fact that you're in the computer age! Do you want to talk to your kids and grandkids intelligently? Then learn the computer. Computers are here to stay and they are not as intimidating as you might suspect. (P.S. I'm writing this book on a computer.)

It is practically an exercise in futility to attempt to list computer programs for Bible study. In our technology-driven culture, knowledge doubles every two years. Quantum leap advancements in this field take place every time we turn around. A program seems outdated almost the moment it hits the market. There are, however, some companies with excellent programs, and they are always developing new ones. Parson's Technology puts together an excellent package called *Quick Verse.* It can stand alone as a Bible search program or you can incorporate their total package, including dictionaries, commentaries, and several other books. Another popular choice is known as *The PC Study Bible.* This is an excellent combination of cross-referencing tools, dictionaries, language helps, and commentaries. Maps and photographs of Bible lands are also included, and they all work interdependently.

If you're ready to move beyond the basic programs, there are many options available on CD ROM. Logos Corporation has developed an intense combination of every imaginable study tool. It is completely searchable—and fast! It's a bit on the pricey side, however, and may not be of interest to the average Bible student.

Let's get back to square one for a moment. The most important item is a good Bible—one that you'll read, rather than relegate to the coffee table for pressing flowers! Remember, you can buy the best Bible study tools available and still not be a good Bible student. As one person put it, "There is no substitute for reading the Bible; it throws a great deal of light on the commentaries!" My travels to third-world countries have led me to believe that having a huge library of books for effective Bible study is not the most important thing in life. I have been amazed by the quality of Christian life in many of the places I have visited—and all without computer technology. In some places, if the people were well-off, they might have had a study Bible like a

Thompson Chain Reference, a concordance, and perhaps a Bible dictionary. Three or four books at most! And I'm talking about pastors and church leaders. Most of these pastors learn how to *inductively* study the Scriptures on their own rather than relying on commentaries and many of the other tools they can't get their hands on. That's one of the aims of this book—to make room for the Holy Spirit to teach you His truth by making key observations and applying them to your life. That's where it's at! Above everything else, when we study God's book, we must make a commitment to be doers of the Word. As Will H. Houghton said so well, "Lay hold on the Bible until the Bible lays hold on you."

How Do I Go About It?

All right, I have the Bible, my notebook is opened, and I'm ready to dive in. What next? How much should I read and, once I read it, what should I do about it? These are good questions, but let me ask you one—Are you hungry? Spiritual hunger is the driving force of effective Bible study.

Sometimes after giving a sermon I am asked, "How can I get more out of my own personal study? After hearing your teaching, I realized that although I've read the passage several times, I've missed so much." The hunger for getting more out of our reading of the Scripture is a healthy sign which God will reward. The first thing to realize is that there is a big difference between *reading* the Scripture and *feeding* on the Scripture.

Martin Luther said he studied the Bible the way he gathered apples. First, he shook the whole tree so that the ripest might fall, then he climbed the tree and shook each limb. When he had shaken each limb, he shook each branch, then every twig and, finally, he looked under each leaf. Let us search the Bible as a whole, shaking the tree by reading it as rapidly as we would any other book, then shaking every limb, studying book after book. We should then shake every branch, giving attention to the chapters (when they do not break the meaning), and then shake every twig by careful study of the paragraphs and sentences. You will be rewarded if you will look under every leaf by searching for the meaning of the words. Looking at the Bible from the "bird's-eye view" down to the "worm's-eye view" provides a great balance. Now let's take a look at several effective methods of studying the Bible.

Devotional Bible Study

Devotional Bible study is the process of reflecting on a few verses or passages of the Scripture and immediately making personal application. Christians typically refer to this as "quiet time" or "having devotions." This can be done on your own simply by selecting a method of reading the Bible through and then reflecting on its truths. This is not so much an academic approach as an applicational approach (although the two can be combined). Rather than examining the Bible as a textbook, as one would in school, we read and study because it is a means to an appointed end—*to encounter God!* We are seeking the Lord and desiring to know His will as it applies to us. The knowledge of the book is not the preeminent goal. We are more interested in knowing the author of the book. With this approach, the time spent in Bible study becomes a joyful rendezvous with our God. It's best to carve out about 30 minutes to an hour each day to meet with God and have Bible reading and prayer.

Aids to a devotional approach include books that will take you through a portion of Scripture every day of the year. *Our Daily Bread* and *The Daily Life* are examples of publications which provide suggested Scripture readings along with brief narratives and devotional thoughts. Other devotional books, like Oswald Chamber's *My Utmost For His Highest*, or Spurgeon's *Morning and Evening*, focus on one verse followed by a full devotional for the day. These publications are excellent and meaningful, however, if you stop there you'll cheat yourself out of digging into the meat of the Word on your own. Don't let this be your only way of reading the Bible.

Verse-By-Verse Bible Study

The most effective way to study the Bible is to go through the Scriptures chapter by chapter, verse by verse, and word by word—all 66 books. I'm not advocating doing this in one sitting, although people have done it. Systematic reading of about 4 chapters of the Bible per day, would result in reading through the entire Bible in 9 or 10 months. Many Bibles have a daily schedule in the back that will provide a good approach to your reading. It is sad that many of God's people have never read the entire Bible, even once. Clearly, we can derive much from this type of study. We get a balanced view of Scripture, and this helps us avoid the common problem of becoming an off-balance Christian.

I suggest a simple plan. Each day pick up where you left off the day before. Some prefer to read straight through, chapter by chapter. Others follow along in a reading program with their local church. If you're still looking for a plan, let me suggest the following:

- *Sunday:* Read whatever portion your church is reading.
- *Monday:* Read from the Legal Books (Genesis to Deuteronomy).
- *Tuesday:* Read from the Historical Books (Joshua to Esther).
- *Wednesday:* Read from the Poetical Books (Job to the Song of Solomon).
- *Thursday:* Read from the Prophetic Books (Isaiah to Malachi).
- *Friday:* Read from the Gospel Books (Matthew, Mark, Luke, and John).

- *Saturday:* Read from the rest of the New Testament (from Acts to Revelation).

Using this method, you can consistently read through the Bible, covering as much ground as you like, taking long or short portions. Place a marker wherever you stop that day and pick it up the next week on the same day. This will allow enough variety in your Bible reading to keep you going and looking forward to the next session.

Systematic Bible Study

Another approach to Bible study is to settle on one idea or topic and systematically study what the Bible has to say on that topic. For example, to study "grace" you would use a concordance to find every instance the word "grace" is found and follow each reference all the way through the Bible. By concentrating more on the singular topic than a systematic verse-by-verse study, you will thoroughly study a few verses at a time and focus on personal application. This allows you to cover some of the essential points of biblical truth and observe some subjects that are of interest to you. This can be helpful to get a more "in-depth" look at Bible themes, but it's also easy to get a bit imbalanced. Why? Simply because in choosing topics that are important to you, you may only look up what suits your fancy and neglect lots of other important "stuff." This approach should be used the way you might order an appetizer in a restaurant: It's a great way to whet the appetite so you can enjoy a full meal of more intense and thorough study.

The Combination of Methods

Over the years, I have used a book called *Search the Scriptures* by Intervarsity Press that has helped me combine all of these methods. Starting with the New Testament book of Luke, this devotional guide follows with an Old Testament book, and then goes back to finish the book of Luke. By reading a portion of the Scripture every day and studying a series of questions to bring out the meaning and relevance of what you have read, the Bible can be fully read in five years. That's not bad, considering the interpretation and application that would be made along the way. It's great to combine a devotional approach with a through-the-Bible approach and throw in a few systematic side trips along the way.

John DeVries, the director of international ministries for the World Home Bible League, has devised a six-point plan for getting something out of almost any passage of Scripture. It can make your Bible reading time an opportunity to enjoy God and His message and not be overwhelmed with principles and interpretations. Read a passage of Scripture and then ask yourself these questions:

1. What did I like?
2. What did I not like?

3. What did I not understand?
4. What did I learn about God?
5. What should I do?
6. What phrase can I take with me today?

Making Time For Bible Study

About now, you may be thinking, "This all sounds great, but who's got that kind of time?" It's true, time is a precious commodity these days. Our schedules are already overloaded with work, family and friends, sleep, and recreation. But have you noticed that we tend to make time for the things that are truly important to us? Somehow we manage to have hobbies, see movies, and go to sporting events. Our days are quickly filled with scheduled events and meetings with all sorts of "important" people. Do yourself a favor—schedule an appointment with God every day. Write it in your daily planner if you need to. He's a pretty important person. Let's make that meeting a priority. When it gets down to it, we can live more simply by stripping ourselves of a lot of activities that really are not as important as they might seem. In 1989, Americans purchased Harlequin romance novels at the rate of 7,191 per hour. If only God's people would show a similar interest in His Word! Let me be frank: If you're too busy to spend time with God—*you're too busy!*

As we read and feed on the Word of God, we should remember the real goal of studying the Bible is not interpretation but in application. It's not just in finding a new tidbit of knowledge about prophecy or the shade of meaning in a Greek word. The joy comes in finding the truth to apply to our own lives. It's then we can see that the Bible works! What a tragic loss when Christians use the Bible merely as decoration, instead of turning it loose to work in their own lives.

I would like a job as tutor, teacher and advisor to your family. I will never take a vacation. I will never be out of humor.

I don't drink or smoke. I won't borrow your clothes or raid your refrigerator.

I will be up in the morning as early as anyone in the household and will stay up as late as anyone wishes.

I will help solve any problems your children might have. I will give you the satisfaction of knowing that no question your children ask will go unanswered. For that matter, I will answer any of your own questions on subjects that range from "How did we get here?" to "Where are we headed?"

I will help settle bets and differences of opinion. I will give you information that will help you with your job, your family, and all of your other interests. In short, I will give you the knowledge that will insure the continued success of your family.

I am your Bible. Do I get the job?

3

Open Your Eyes

Scripture knowledge is the candle without which faith cannot see to do its work. —Anonymous

The Bible has been around for a long time, and it's still a best-seller. Every year, more copies of the Scriptures are printed than in the previous year. Although this may sound encouraging, don't get too excited. Lots of folks figure they should buy a Bible and maybe even look at it from time to time, but it seems that many don't know much about what's inside. While the Bible is the most outstanding piece of literature ever written, many "enlightened" Americans know little or nothing about it.

A few years ago, five classes of high school seniors were tested on their knowledge of common Bible themes. Most of them completely failed the exam. Some were so confused they thought Sodom and Gomorrah were lovers, and the gospels were written by Matthew, Mark, Luther (instead of Luke), and John. Others said that Eve was created from an apple and that the stories Jesus used in teaching were called "parodies." More than eighty percent of the pupils could not complete such familiar quotations as, "Many are called but few are (chosen)," or "a soft answer turns away (wrath)."

Certainly, these are honest mistakes. No one can be expected to remember every detail of every Bible story. Not even the most mature Christian is a walking concordance! But the greater point here is one of *observation*. Many people who read the Bible simply don't see it—that is, they are not making notable observations about it. We've all experienced this when meeting someone new. We smile, shake hands, exchange names, discuss bits of information, smile a bit more, and then go our way. If, later, someone asked us to describe the person we just met, we'd have a hard time accurately recalling his appearance. There might be certain features we could remember, but unless we made mental notes of his clothing, facial features, and hair style we'd be hard pressed to give a composite description. We were there. We saw. We spoke. We pressed palms. But we didn't observe.

Three Steps to Understanding

If you have a sincere desire to study the Bible, there are several approaches you might consider. All of them are valid and each has its place. You could try a formal approach, such as attending a Bible school, which allows the student to take a variety of courses and study intensely. Some get so serious, they may even go on to seminary. If the teachers are stimulating, it can be an exciting environment. Many find it fulfilling to walk the great halls of academia and fill their minds with lofty knowledge. For most people, however, this option isn't feasible because it's expensive and time consuming. I know what you're thinking—since it's the study of the Scriptures, it's worth the time and cash. I agree. However, there are limitations to studying the Bible this way—not everyone can do it.

Others choose the less formal path. Correspondence courses, weekly study groups, and seminars can provide many insights into the Bible, adding to your learning. Those who get involved feel they're a part of something, and as long as they do their homework, everything is okay.

Many others take a totally unstructured approach to Bible study. It amounts to little more than *reading* and *raking*—letting one's mind comb through the stories and keeping whatever it retains for that day—the rest is lost. Whatever rises to the surface in the course of their regular reading is grasped. While it's possible to learn in this manner, much is missed or lost along the way.

Let me suggest another approach. It can be done in a classroom setting, through a correspondence course, or on your own as you sit quietly with your Bible in hand. This is a method of personal study which will enable you to look deeply at Scripture, understand what you have read, and then take what you have learned and apply it to your life. Anyway, that's what it's all about, right? To do this, you will learn to use the principles of *observation, interpretation,* and *application:*

Observation is *opening your eyes* to what the text is saying.

Interpretation is *opening your mind* to what the text means.

Application is *opening your heart* to discover what the passage means to you personally and applying it to your daily life.

It All Begins With Prayer

Just because we can read and retain information, when it comes to the Bible, we dare not be presumptuous. This is God's book and the Holy Spirit must bring illumination of its truths to our hearts. That's why the first step of study is prayer. Even David (who wrote a good chunk of Scripture himself) saw this need. In Psalm 119 he prayed, "Open my eyes, that I may see wondrous things from Your law" (Psalm 119:18). Ask God to open your eyes and your mind to His Word. You could begin your study with a prayer something like this, "Lord, I now submit myself to You, as Your vessel. I pray that You would speak to me personally about the important issues I may be neglecting that concern my own life. Lord, I give you complete permission to investigate and search my heart to see if there is anything in me that is lacking. Challenge me on any issue and comfort me with Your promises. In Jesus' name, amen."

In the course of your study, you'll come to tough passages—difficult portions of Scripture that you don't understand. Stop again, and pray for insight and wisdom. Cry out for light and understanding. Following your time of Bible study, thank God for the insight He has given you. This way, your whole session of Bible study will have been bathed in prayer. By presenting yourself to God as an empty vessel, eager to be filled, you have taken the single most effective step in understanding and applying the truths of the Bible. The great preacher R.W. Dale noted that, "Study without prayer is atheism, and prayer without study is presumption." We need both prayer and study. What God has joined together, let not any man separate.

What Shall I Observe?
Observe Text and Context

The *text* refers to the actual Bible passage we are considering, and *context* refers to what is with or around the text. This is the first rule in finding out the meaning of any passage of Scripture. Failing to consider context is perhaps the most common cause for misunderstanding the Scriptures. Many people know the following verse: "For God so loved the world that He gave His only begotten Son, that whoever believes in Him should not perish but have everlasting life" (John 3:16). The *text* is this specific verse, the *context* refers to what is around or with the text. In observing the context of this text, we find that Jesus was speaking to a Pharisee, Nicodemus, about being "born again." Nicodemus was a natural man who struggled with spiritual truths. In addition to the reassuring promise of eternal life found in the passage, when we read on we see that Jesus informed Nicodemus of his responsibility to believe in order to receive the gift of eternal life: "For God did not send his Son into the world to condemn the world, but that the world through Him might be saved. He who believes in Him is not condemned; but he who does not believe is condemned already, because he has not believed in the name of the only begotten Son of God" (John 3:17,18). Jesus not only promised *redemption* for those who choose to believe in Him, but *condemnation* for those who don't. His promise, considered in the context of the surrounding verses, also contained the warning that we are each responsible for our personal choice to believe or not believe.

When you read, consider a couple of things: What is the *immediate context* of this passage and what is the *remote context?* Immediate context is comprised of the verses immediately surrounding the verse or verses being studied. The remote context includes a bit more—the phrase, paragraph, surrounding sentences, or the entire book in which the passage is contained. Many of the great church splits and heresies throughout history have happened because the context simply wasn't considered. Even our efforts to memorize Scripture (as good and productive as that is) are sometimes compromised by the failure to recognize we are memorizing only a portion of the passage, often without consideration of the true context. We tend to isolate a promise and memorize it, sometimes being totally oblivious to the condition that's glued to that promise.

For example, one may single out Philippians 4:19 as a promise for anyone. The verse states, "And my God shall supply all your need according to His riches in glory by Christ Jesus." It is an awesome promise indeed. But is this promise given to any believer to use anytime he wants to get whatever he thinks he needs? That's how many Christians use it. When we dig deeper, however, we find that this verse doesn't stand by itself. It has a context—other verses that set forth its meaning. Paul was writing to a group of believers who had sacrificially given to the Lord's work. They deeply cared for Paul and wanted to share in getting the gospel out by supporting his ministry of evangelism. It wasn't easy for them to do this, but they considered it an important investment. Notice the *immediate context* for this verse:

Nevertheless you have done well that you shared in my distress. Now you Philippians know also that in the beginning of the gospel, when I departed from Macedonia, no church shared with me concerning giving and receiving but you only. For even in Thessalonica you sent aid once and again for my necessities. Not that I seek the gift, but I seek the fruit that abounds to your account. Indeed I have all and abound. I am full, having received from Epaphroditus the things which were sent from you, a sweet-smelling aroma, an acceptable sacrifice, well pleasing to God. And my God shall supply all your need according to His riches in glory by Christ Jesus. (Phil. 4:14-19)

A different picture is painted when this verse is observed in context. The promise is that God will supply the needs of those who have sacrificially stood behind the work of God through the support of His servants. It's the same principle Jesus gave to His disciples in Matthew 6:33, "But seek first the kingdom of God and His righteousness, and all these things shall be added to you." The context provides the setting in which the promise is to be applied.

Observe From A Bird's-Eye View

There is nothing like seeing the Grand Canyon from twenty thousand feet in the air. In the context of the surrounding landscape, the enormity of this chasm is dramatically displayed. I appreciate it much more up close because of the perspective of having seen it from far away. In chapter two, I mentioned that Martin Luther liked to get this large view first when studying the Word of God. Using the analogy of the tree, he first shook the whole tree, that the ripest fruit might fall. Then he climbed the tree and shook each limb. When he had shaken each limb, he shook each branch and, finally, he looked under each leaf.

Before going into detailed study, the whole book should be observed from a broad perspective. The best way to do this is to read, in one sitting, the entire book of the Bible we are studying. In the shorter New Testament books or the Minor Prophets of the Old Testament, this isn't a problem—they're nice and *concise*. But there are some books that are much longer and more formidable. To read Isaiah at one sitting would require a huge chunk of time or an Evelyn Wood speed-reading course. So let me suggest another way to get a broad perspective with the larger books. Try reading just the headings and first sentences of each section. This will enable you to catch the atmosphere of what the book is about, how it flows, and where it is going. This is like seeing the Bible from twenty thousand feet— you'll be able to observe the general terrain and the major landmarks of each book of the Bible. You'll taxi through the introduction, take off in the first few chapters, and soar over the main body of the text. By the time you land with the closing chapter, you'll have a feel for the entire message. It may be a quick flight, but a lot of information can be gleaned in this way before you walk over the terrain more slowly.

Observe From a Journalist's-Eye View: Who? What? When? Where? Why? and How?

Journalists use these six questions: "Who, What, When, Where, Why, and How?" to uncover a story and then to accurately write and convey it. When we take these same questions into the study of the Bible, we will discover facts which lead us to a deeper understanding of the passage. Now, it isn't necessary to find the answers to all six questions in every passage but simply as many as possible. It will be a rewarding exercise. Once we begin this process, it becomes almost automatic and increases one's depth of study and breadth of understanding.

Let's try it. The first 20 verses of the Gospel of Mark is a great place to start. Let's read it through and then ask these basic questions.

The beginning of the gospel of Jesus Christ, the Son of God. As it is written in the Prophets: "Behold, I send My messenger before Your face, Who will prepare Your way before You. The voice of one crying in the wilderness: 'Prepare the way of the Lord, make His paths straight.'" John came baptizing in the wilderness and preaching a baptism of repentance for the remission of sins. And in all the land of Judea, and those from Jerusalem, went out to him and were all baptized by him in the Jordan River, confessing their sins. Now John was clothed with camel's hair and with a leather belt around his waist, and he ate locusts and wild honey. And he preached, saying, "There comes One after me who is mightier than I, whose sandal strap I am not worthy to stoop down and loose. I indeed baptized you with water, but He will baptize you with the Holy Spirit." It came to pass in those days that Jesus came from Nazareth of Galilee, and was baptized by John in the Jordan. And immediately, coming up from the water, He saw the heavens parting and the Spirit descending upon Him like a dove. Then a voice came from heaven, "You are My beloved Son, in whom I am well pleased." And immediately the Spirit drove Him into the wilderness. And He was there in the wilderness forty days, tempted by Satan, and was with the wild beasts; and the angels ministered to Him. Now after John was put in prison, Jesus came to Galilee, preaching the gospel of the kingdom of God, and saying, "The time is fulfilled, and the kingdom of God is at hand. Repent, and believe in the gospel." And as He walked by the Sea of Galilee, He saw Simon and Andrew his brother casting a net into the sea; for they were fishermen. Then Jesus said to them, "Come after Me, and I will make you become fishers of men." And immediately they left their nets and followed Him. When he had gone a little farther from there, He saw James the son of Zebedee, and John his brother, who also were in the boat mending their nets. And immediately He called them, and they left their father Zebedee in the boat with the hired servants, and went after Him. (Mark 1:1-20)

That's the text. Now, let's begin the questioning process asking, Who? What? When? Where? Why? and How?

Who was involved in this passage? There were lots of people: John the Baptist, Jesus, Simon, Andrew, angels, the voice of the Father, and the Spirit. We also have James, John, and their father, Zebedee. If we were to investigate the identity of each person and his reason for being included in this passage, it would take us further along the path of observation. We see that, from the beginning, the ministry of Jesus included many people. He came to touch people's lives, and the lives He touched were those of the common people—fishermen.

Next, *what* is the literary form of the passage? Was

it a narrative, or poetry such as in the book of Psalms? Was it prophetic like the book of Daniel? Was it didactic, meaning pure teaching like Jesus' Sermon on the Mount? This passage is a narrative—Mark is simply telling the story. He vividly paints his story so his readers will understand easily. His style is swift. It seems he wanted to plant as many visual images as possible.

When did all this take place? At the "beginning of the gospel of Jesus Christ" (vs. 1). Mark is showing how it all started. It began according to the prophecies of Isaiah, with a forerunner named John, who pointed to the coming of Jesus. There was a baptism at this same time (vs.9), and notice the wording of verse 12, "immediately the Spirit drove Him into the wilderness." There was no time wasted.

God had a timetable to keep and that included temptations. We also notice the exact time when Jesus began proclaiming His message. It was "after John was put in prison" (vs. 14). So we see that when John's voice was silenced, the Messiah's voice was heard.

Where did this incident take place? It took place first at the Jordan River, then the scene shifted to the wilderness of Judea and, finally, it ended at the Sea of Galilee. A lot of territory is covered in just 20 verses, which tells us that it is a rapidly moving narrative. These are just first impressions and general observations we can make from asking questions about a section or verses.

Why did Mark write this account? Are there any clues here? One would actually need to read the entire gospel to answer this question, but there are hints in this passage. In the first verse, Mark begins with a declaration of faith that Jesus Christ is the Son of God. He wants us to know that he believes Jesus to be the promised Messiah, the One who is also God's Son. Throughout the book, he makes mention of the reaction of the people to Jesus; that they were astonished at Him. It seems obvious that he wrote this to help us discover what those who saw and heard Him had already discovered—Jesus was no ordinary man. Jesus wasn't just a good man. He was the God-Man!

How does Mark's account contribute to the story of Jesus Christ? This may be harder to discover, but a little patience and keen observation will help. The word "immediately" is used several times in these few verses (vss. 10, 12, 18, and 20). This happens to be a pattern of writing that is peculiar to Mark. Notice that he begins many of his sentences with words like, "then" and "now." Reading a narrative with this kind of language structure, one gets the idea of constant action. When we notice these subtleties, we get the notion that Mark is portraying Jesus as a servant who is always on the go, always concerned about doing the will of His Father in Heaven.

By asking investigative questions, we gain insight into what the Holy Spirit was trying to convey through the original authors of the Bible. This is part of the *illumination* process—the Spirit of God revealing the Word of God to the people of God.

Observe From a Worm's-Eye View

Going from a bird's-eye view to a worm's-eye view requires looking closely at certain details that would be missed by a quick scan. Birds and worms may see the same things *generally*, but their views are much different *specifically*.

Observe Repeated Words and Phrases

There are other structural and stylistic patterns that help us understand the author's meaning and emphasis. Looking at this text from Mark, we find the words "gospel" and "preaching" repeated three times each in these 20 verses. Think about the word "preach." The Bible dictionary tells us it means to "herald or proclaim," and in this context, John the Baptist was heralding and proclaiming the good news of Jesus Christ—the gospel. After John was silenced, Jesus also started preaching. Later, the followers of Jesus did the same. At the end of the book, they will be told to proclaim it to the whole world.

Further observation will reveal that the word "immediately" is a key to the gospel of Mark. We've already noticed this as we asked the *how* question above. We remarked that this is a stylistic quality of Mark's authorship depicting the flow and intensity of the life of Jesus.

Observe Peculiar Words

As you read, you'll notice authors using words that we don't understand or words we don't use on an everyday basis. They may have been words that were understandable to the ancient Jewish culture more than to a post-modern American culture. This is where a Bible dictionary, or a even a plain old English dictionary, will come in handy. In the verses at hand, the word "repentance" might be an unusual word to us. Many in our society don't have a clue as to what that means, but it's used here:

John came baptizing in the wilderness and preaching a baptism of repentance for the remission of sins. (Mark 1:4)

Americans don't talk much about repentance, so it is possible that in reading this passage for the first time we might not know what it means. We might conjure up images of wearing sackcloth and ashes, fasting, or taking long barefoot walks in the desert. So, it would be helpful to look up the word in a Bible dictionary. In it we find an entire summary of "repentance" as found in the Old and New Testaments, as well as the Hebrew and Greek words and how the word came about. The following is a portion of the Bible dictionary definition:

In the New Testament, the word translated "repent" in Greek usually means to change one's mind; to regret or to feel remorse. The best trans-

lation is "metanoeo," which means to turn around.

That clears a lot of mental fog from the subject, doesn't it? We begin to understand that "repentance" is an active word involving both the heart and outward actions. It means to change one's mind about Jesus and to change one's actions accordingly. Noticing these peculiar words and looking them up allows us to accurately understand their meaning.

In verse four, repentance is also mentioned in the immediate context of the remission of sins. "Remission" is another word we might need to look up. It may or may not be in the Bible dictionary, so we could look for it in an English dictionary (Webster's will often give the original root meaning of a word). In *Webster's Ninth New Collegiate Dictionary*, remission is defined: "to remit; to send back; or to release the guilt or the penalty of sin."

In studying the definitions of these two "peculiar" words, we have not only gained insight into some fundamental concepts of salvation, we have also answered the reason "why" John the Baptist preached and "why" Jesus came into the world. They came to deal with the sin problem that has plagued mankind from the beginning.

Observe Comparisons and Contrasts

To see something more clearly, it often helps to compare it to something else. The computer, for instance, can be taken for granted in our fast-paced age of tech-

nology. However, when compared to the first desk cal-
culator or the first computer from the 1940's which was
the size of an 18 wheel diesel rig and weighed more than
17 Chevrolet Cameros, you can truly appreciate the
wonder of the modern laptop! The same holds true in
the Bible. There are comparisons to be found in these
verses as well. Notice verses 2 and 3:

> *As it is written in the Prophets: "Behold, I send*
> *My messenger before Your face, Who will prepare*
> *your way before You. The voice of one crying in*
> *the wilderness: 'Prepare the way of the Lord,*
> *make His paths straight.'" (Mark 1:2, 3)*

Here we find a comparison between the "messenger"
and the "Lord." The messenger isn't the Lord, but rather
the one pointing the way to the Lord. John the Baptist
made that distinction when he declared that he was the
"messenger" who wasn't even worthy to stoop down and
loosen the sandals of the Lord. The Lord is vibrantly
seen against the background of His "messenger."

Now, look at another instance of contrast in verse 13:

> *And He was there in the wilderness forty days,*
> *tempted by Satan, and was with the wild beasts;*
> *and the angels ministered to Him. (Mark 1:13)*

In just one short sentence, we see that contrast within the spirit world in the life of Jesus. While He was in
the wilderness being tempted by Satan, He was also
receiving the ministry of the angels. The contrast vivid-

ly portrays the conflict of principalities which was laid upon the shoulders of Jesus Christ.

Observe Any Figurative Expressions

Figures of speech are the words that add spice and flavor to language. Virtually every language has them—words and phrases that add color to the mental picture. In everyday speech, we use such expressions all the time. We might say, "His argument doesn't hold water." This is a figurative way of conveying doubt in someone's reasoning process. Sometimes we hear a person say he is "standing on God's Word." Does that mean there's a Bible under his or her feet? No. He is figuratively saying that he is firmly counting on what God has said in the Bible. In the Bible there are also examples of figurative expressions. Our text in Mark has a couple that are obvious:

> And he preached, saying, "There comes One after me who is mightier than I, whose sandal strap I am not worthy to stoop down and loose." (Mark 1:7)

A good Bible dictionary would provide the background of this custom: As a gesture of hospitality, when a guest entered the house, the servant would stoop to untie his sandals. John is figuratively saying that he is not even worthy to be Jesus' servant. Even the lowest place in the house is too high for John to occupy because Jesus is so exalted. There is another figurative expression in these verses:

Then Jesus said to them, "Come after Me, and I will make you become fishers of men." (Mark 1:17)

Did Jesus mean that they would literally walk around hooking people with a fishing pole and reeling them in? Were the disciples to take their nets to entangle people so they could preach to them? Obviously not. This is another figurative expression to which the people could relate. They were familiar with catching fish for their livelihood. When they chose to follow Jesus, they would figuratively cast out their nets to draw men and women to God. Jesus meant that there would be a change in the very drive of their existence. No longer would they be so concerned with their occupations, for they had been given a higher one—catching the souls of men and women.

Observe Any Strange Things

There are many strange things in the Bible. Consider John the Baptist—anything strange about him? When was the last time you saw anyone come to church wearing a camel's hair tunic cinched with a leather belt? How often do you meet people who live out in the desert and feed on locusts? When we identify the "strange things" in a passage, we are often able to focus on unique events and the truths.

Looking at a Bible atlas or map, we might think it strange that Jesus was at the Jordan River. The center of Judaism was in Jerusalem, and here He was about 30 miles away in a dry, dusty area about 1,250 feet below sea level. Why did John come there to baptize rather than to one of the other pools such as Bethesda or Siloam? People had to trek from the cities to the middle of nowhere to see Him. Are these important questions? We really don't know until we dig deeper. Careful observation will teach us to look for these kinds of things. This is the challenge and fun of personal Bible study.

Observe By Picturing Yourself There

A technique that has helped me study the Scripture more than any single thing, is trying to place myself into the text. By picturing the scene and getting behind the words, I begin to see things as they were when the author was inspired to write. I ask myself to whom the letter or book was addressed; what problems were they facing; what was the purpose of the writing; and other questions as they occur to me. Then I place myself in the crowd. I'm wearing an ancient tunic and I'm traveling towards Jerusalem. Suddenly, my curiosity compels me to find out why a crowd has gathered down by the Jordan river.

You Are There

Picture yourself in the midst of a crowd gathered in a remote, desert area. It's hot and dusty. As you make your way through the masses, you look down to see a wild-looking character dunking people in the murky waters. He is a crudely dressed fellow. As he approaches, you see that he has long hair, indicating he has taken the vow of the Nazarite, and he is dressed in camel's hair. He speaks boldly, like no one you have ever heard. You are stunned when he says, "Repent!" What thoughts go through your mind? How do you personally react to these words? Will you go down into the water as well?

John tells the crowd that there is One coming whose sandal strap he is unworthy to loosen. Unlike himself, the One who comes will baptize, not with water but with the Holy Spirit. Your eye is then caught by the man walking toward John. It's a man named Jesus. After picturing this dramatic scene and meditating on it, read the passage again and ask the questions we have discussed. Soon, through this process of observation and investigation, the Scripture seems to come alive and you will understand the impact of the words in a new way.

Every spring, bees and butterflies emerge seeking nourishment from flowers. The butterfly darts here and there and sips only the external sweets. The bee, however, goes deeper. Even if the flower is closed, the industrious little insect is not deterred. He pushes his way in until he finds the hidden, but luscious, nectar. In your study of God's sweet Word, dive and dig until you've tasted of every last drop of spiritual nectar and are satisfied by its sweetness.

I love the way A. B. Simpson put Bible study in perspective when he wrote the following:

God has hidden every precious thing in such a way that it is a reward to the diligent, a prize to the earnest, but a disappointment to the slothful soul. All nature is arrayed against the lounger and the idler. The nut is hidden in its thorny case; the pearl is buried beneath the ocean waves; the gold is imprisoned in the rocky bosom of the mountains; the gem is found only after you crush the rock which encloses it; the very soil gives its harvest as a reward to the laboring farmer. So truth and God must be earnestly sought.

It was Henry Ford who was credited with saying, "Cut your own wood and you warm yourself twice." He meant that the man who chops his own firewood not only enjoys the heat from the logs burning in his fireplace, but he also gets physically warmed from the exercise involved in his labor. Diligent study of God's Word will warm the soul like nothing else can. It will keep the flame of devotion alive as well as fuel your mind to learn more of Him.

Open Your Mind

It is always easier to understand what the Bible says than to understand what somebody thinks it meant to say. —*Vance Havner*

E ver heard someone shoot back this retort when you tried to share a truth of Scripture, "Well, that's *your* interpretation"? When they say something like this, you may stop and wonder, "Are they right? Maybe there are other interpretations of the Bible, and I'm way off track." Certainly, there are disagreements beneath the large umbrella of Christianity, but it's not as bad as some may believe. When it comes to the essentials of the Christian faith, there is unity among believers. Of course, there is lots of room for discussion and disagreement in areas that are non-essential: the precise chronology of the return of Christ, the application of certain spiritual gifts within the church, etc.

We can interpret Scripture by leaning toward our own bias, rather like the attitude of the driver of a tour bus in Nashville, Tennessee. The driver was pointing out the sites of the Civil War Battle of Nashville. He said, "Right over here a small group of Confederate soldiers held off a whole Yankee brigade." A little farther along, he said, "Over there, a young Confederate boy held off a Yankee platoon all by himself." This went on and on until finally a member of the tour group asked, "Didn't the Yankees win anything in the Battle of Nashville?" The bus driver replied, "Not while I'm the driver of this bus, they didn't!"

This is where a good plan of interpretation can come in. By making the right *observations*, you can be reasonably sure that you'll land on the right *interpretation*. There are certain rules to follow so you can be assured of the correct meaning of a Bible passage. We can objectively view the Scriptures and allow the Holy Spirit to drive the bus.

I know, I know—when you come to a chapter like this one, you may think, "This isn't all that important. All I have to do is read my Bible and listen to whatever a pastor or TV evangelist tells me, and I'll be fine." Wrong! You may end up so totally confused that you won't know which end is up. Just because someone can talk in front of a camera doesn't mean he is saying all the right things. Interpretation is essential in studying God's revelation. *You* must study to show *yourself* approved unto God so that you can rightly divide the word of truth (2 Tim. 2:15). These days, there are too many predators in the pulpit and too much passivity in the pew! One way to boost your discernment is to learn how to interpret Scripture for yourself. Dave Hunt and T.A. McMahon remind us of the importance of this in their fine book, *The Seduction of Christianity:*

> *Christianity may well be facing the greatest challenge in its history: a series of powerful and growing seductions that are subtly changing biblical interpretations and undermining the faith of millions of people. Most Christians are scarcely aware of what is happening, and much less do they understand the issues involved.*
>
> *The seduction is surprisingly easy. It does not take place as an obvious frontal assault from rival religious beliefs. That would be vigorously resisted. Instead, it comes to some Christians in the guise of faith-producing techniques for gaining spiritual power and experiencing miracles and to others as self-improvement psychologies for fully realizing human potential that are seen as scientific aids to successful Christian living.*

It takes personal knowledge and understanding of the Scriptures to ward off these subtle attacks. Don't get me wrong—there are many difficult passages that are tough to understand and interpret. It may feel as though we are wading through deep rivers. After all, this is God's Word we're dealing with—it's not lightweight stuff! Even the great D. L. Moody said:

I am glad there's a depth in the Bible I know nothing about, for it shows its Divine authorship. A man once came to me with a very difficult passage and said, "Mr. Moody, how do you explain that?" I replied, "I don't." "But how do you interpret it?" "I don't interpret it." "Well, how do you understand it?" "I don't understand it." "What do you do with it?" "I believe it! I believe many things I don't understand." In John 3, Jesus reminded Nicodemus that if he was unable to grasp earthly things, heavenly things would be far beyond him. Nature itself is filled with wonders we cannot fathom, so how can we expect to know everything spiritual?

Still, God has spoken so that we can understand. Keep in mind that it's God's delight to reveal and enlighten. He loves His children to understand His ways. Moses said:

The secret things belong to the LORD our God, but those things which are revealed belong to us and to our children forever, that we may do all the words of this law. (Deut. 29:29)

Whenever we look for the interpretation of a passage, our purpose is simply to find out what the author *originally intended* the hearers or readers to understand. In the previous chapter, we learned that observation means to open our eyes to what the text is saying by getting an over-all perspective, asking pertinent questions, and making observations. Now we learn about opening our minds to the meaning of those observations. Don't worry! Interpretation doesn't have to be an intimidating process. Our time spent on observation has laid a foundation of facts for us to build on using methods leading to interpretation and understanding. There are a few rules to follow that will help us understand the exact meaning of any passage.

Shedding Light On Interpretation
Principle #1: *What is the Context?*

The first thing to do when looking at a passage of Scripture is to see what is *around* the passage—the other verses of Scripture. These verses are the *context* in which the *text* is found; the connective fiber for the verse. Look at the verses that precede and follow the passage. A good practice is to trace the passage's "thread of thought." Find where the author introduces the thought and track it to its conclusion. You will find that many passages have an entirely different meaning in context than when isolated from it. Anyone can make the Bible say almost anything if they choose. For instance, I could quote from the Bible and tell you, "There is no God." But if I quote the entire verse the meaning becomes plain, "The fool has said in his heart, 'There is no God'" (Ps. 53:1). When the phrase is seen in the context of the entire verse, it means the exact

59

opposite. Granted, that was a rather simplistic example, but the principle is the same whether it's a word, phrase, or paragraph. The true meaning of a verse is the one provided by its context. Most false doctrines and aberrant teachings arise from neglecting this principle. To put it another way, "Any text without a context will become a pretext."

There are two levels of context to keep in mind—immediate context and remote context. Immediate context refers to the sentence in which a word is found or the paragraph in which a sentence is found. It is what is close by the passage at hand. Remote context refers to the entire thought process of the verse. For example, let's look at a familiar passage:

Therefore we also, since we are surrounded by so great a cloud of witnesses, let us lay aside every weight, and the sin which so easily ensnares us, and let us run with endurance the race that is set before us. (Heb. 12:1)

The immediate context of the verse would be the first two verses in that chapter. It refers to a race of faith that is to be run with endurance. The verses speak of how to run that race and who to keep our eyes on while we run. But the remote context takes a broader scope. The thought can be traced back to the beginning of the eleventh chapter. There, several examples of faith are given as portrayed by the saints through the ages. The first word of chapter twelve is "therefore." This word connects the thought of the race with the previous examples of faith. The "cloud of witnesses" refers to the list of the faithful people from the previous chapter. The passage is reminiscent of the athletic events of ancient Greece and Rome. Former participants are present as witnesses. Warm-up weights are representative of sin, which is to be laid aside in the serious competition of life. Life is a race in which the believer is asked to "run with endurance."

Principle #2: *What Do the Words Mean?*

Just about everyone uses words as the primary way to communicate. Our ability to articulate in language distinguishes us from other living creatures. There is no parallel in the animal world, as speech is uniquely human. In fact, the average person spends about one fifth of his/her life talking. In your lifetime, you will use enough words to fill a library of three thousand large volumes totaling approximately one million, five hundred thousand words!

Since the Bible was written by stringing words together to form coherent thoughts, we must make our interpretation based on the words used. This seems obvious and easy enough, however, there are some problems. Some words have more than one meaning. If I say "light," you may not know exactly what I mean. Am I referring to the electromagnetic waves emanating from the sun? Do I mean the opposite of heavy? Perhaps I am trying to describe the shade of a color. The Bible uses "light" in much the same manner. It may refer to the light of the sun as in Genesis when God said, "'Let there be light'; and there was light"(Gen. 1:3). Or it may carry a figurative connotation as in the words of Simeon when he saw the Christ child and declared Him to be, "A light to bring revelation to the Gentiles, and the glory of Your people Israel." It could also mean to deem something as unimportant. Jesus used it this way when He told the parable of the wedding feast and described the response of those who refused to come by saying, "But they made light of it and went their ways, one to his own farm, another to his business" (Matt. 22:5). Usually, the context will clear things up in such cases.

Language is fluid, with words and meanings changing over time. In the old days, the word "conversation" meant something entirely different than it does today. In Hebrews 13:5 the King James translation is, "Let your conversation be without covetousness" which sounds like it means that, when you speak, you shouldn't reveal your desires. But that is not the meaning of the verse. A more modern rendering would be, "Let your *conduct* be without covetousness." Why the change? Simply because the word meaning itself has changed. Once upon a time "conversation" meant "conduct" or "one's manner of life." Over time, the meaning has changed.

To understand the words used in a passage, we must observe how they fit into the context. Look up some of them in the dictionary. Since words often have more than one meaning, find out the variations. Some words can be found in a Bible dictionary which will explain their specific meanings in the Old and New Testaments. An *Expository Dictionary of Biblical Words* by W.E. Vine will prove very helpful.

Principle #3: *What Does the Grammar Show?*

I know, I know—right about now you're thinking, "I thought the title of this book said something about ENJOYING Bible study. Now he's talking about grammar? I'm outta here!" Hold on. I'm not trying to conjure up images of your high school English class; I'm simply trying to help you understand what you read. Words are always used in combination with other words. The relationship of those words provides the meaning. What can you tell about a person who shouts out, "Nuts!" Did he hurt himself? Did he forget something? Did he find some acorns on the trail while walking in the woods? We need other words to make the meaning clear. To understand what a person means when he writes or speaks, both parties must have the same understanding of how words relate to one another in the sentences or paragraph. Don't be afraid of words, use them to your advantage.

Stressing the importance of grammar and vocabulary, a high school English teacher told his class, "Use a word ten times, and it will be yours for life." In the back of the room a pretty, blonde senior closed her eyes and chanted under her breath, "Fred, Fred, Fred, Fred, Fred, Fred, Fred, Fred, Fred, Fred."

You don't have to be an English major to understand the Bible. It helps, however, to identify parts of speech: noun, pronoun, verb, adverb, preposition, conjunction, etc. Another thing to look for is how these words relate in the sentence. After the resurrection, Jesus asked Peter, "Simon, son of Jonah, do you love Me more than these?"(John 21:15). What did He mean? Did he love Him more than what—more than whom? The dictionary reveals that "these" is an adjective or a demonstrative pronoun: "being the person, thing, or idea that is present or near in place, time or thought or that has just been mentioned." Well then, what person, thing, or idea was present or had just been mentioned? In the story, the disciple had just been fishing and had caught some fish. Perhaps Jesus was referring to Peter's love for catching fish and, therefore, was asking him about his priorities, as if to say, "Peter, am I more important than your occupation?" Maybe "these" could mean "these other disciples." After all, it was Peter who had earlier boasted that he was more faithful than everyone else. When Jesus predicted that they would all stumble when

He was crucified, Peter piped up, "Even if all are made to stumble because of You, I will never be made to stumble" (Matt. 26:33). That was quite a boast. Maybe Jesus was asking him about that, now that it was over. Can you see how grammar can help you understand the meaning? It may not always be able to convey the exact and undisputed meaning, but it can show you the viable definitions.

When looking at a passage of Scripture, give some attention to the structure. Try to identify the key thought of the verse by first finding the subject and verb. Then notice the relationship of the other words around it. Try to come up with all the possible meanings. If you see more meanings than one, consider the context and the meaning of the words.

Principle #4: *What is the Background?*

Have you ever walked in late to a play or a movie? The plot has already begun to unfold, the key characters have been introduced, and the setting has been revealed. So, when you arrive, you're confused and frustrated because you've missed out on some important information—the background! You wonder, "Who's that character talking about? Why did he say that? What does he mean by that?" Then you frustrate others who have been watching from the beginning by pestering them with questions as they're watching.

Reading a single paragraph or even chapter in the Bible can produce the same effect. We often jump right into the middle of a story and neglect to discover the setting, key characters, customs, and plot. We lift out a text and memorize it without considering the background. When we do, we can fall into the trap of interpreting the passage in the context of our own culture and setting. That's fine when it comes to *application* of the Bible, but we first must see the Bible in its original setting and background.

The Bible has a setting. The events took place within a certain culture—a Semitic culture. The society was mostly agrarian and simple. The cities were compact and had towers, walls, and gates for protection. They generally were on elevated sites with a water source nearby for sustenance and protection. Water didn't come from the tap but was fetched from huge cisterns or wells. The clothing was certainly different. Rather than being purchased from a mall, they were handmade, earthy, and simple. The basic article of clothing was the tunic, to which various accessories were added. The lifestyle, customs, and language, help us understand the setting and meaning of the Bible.

Why is this important? Simply because there were customs and expressions in ancient biblical cultures with which we are totally unfamiliar. An idiom that had meaning in one culture or at one time in history doesn't necessarily have the same meaning in another. Ask any missionary about this. Leaving the comforts of home and going abroad to another culture can be very disorienting. The language is different. So are the customs and the weather, not to mention the food! Once, in the Philippines, I had a funny tasting meat that I courageously inhaled to prove that I could acclimate well. I'll admit, the taste was a bit exotic, but I wasn't going to be deterred. It wasn't until a couple of days later that one of the locals told me I had consumed a fat, juicy wormburger!

When we turn to the pages of Scripture, we find similar cultural gaps that must be noted and understood. For example, when we read of the man who came to Jesus wanting first to go and "bury his father" we might be a bit put off by Jesus' terse response. He told this young man, "Follow Me, and let the dead bury their own dead." What? How insensitive can Jesus be? But that expression "bury my father" did not mean that his father was already dead. The phrase was a common Near Eastern figure of speech that referred to a son's responsibility to help his father in the family business until the father died and the inheritance was distributed. Well, that could involve a long period of time— many years if the father was still young and in good health. That idiom is still used in parts of the Middle East today.

A few years ago, a missionary asked a rich young Turkish man to go with him on a trip to Europe, during which time the missionary hoped to disciple the man. When the young man replied that he must bury his father, the missionary offered his sympathy and expressed surprise that the father had died. The man told him that his father was alive and healthy. He explained that the expression "bury my father" meant staying at home and fulfilling his family responsibilities until his father died and he received his share of the inheritance. So, what this man was saying to Jesus was equivalent to, "I want to wait until I receive my inheritance."

Another example of the importance of background in the Bible is found in John 13 when Jesus washed the disciples' feet at the Last Supper. He then told them to do the same to others. Does that mean Christians ought to pull the socks off other Christians and scrub away? The background of the culture gives us a clue. Before meals were eaten, the hands were always washed under running water because there were no utensils such as knives, forks, and spoons. In a wealthy home this task would be performed by a servant. By New Testament times, this had become something of a ritual. Under certain conditions, servants would wash the feet of guests who had just come into the house after walking the dusty Middle Eastern roads. Jesus took on the role of a servant in washing the feet, but not the hands, of the disciples at the Last Supper. He was telling His followers to be willing to take the lowest place among others—that of a servant.

The same principle holds true today in many cultures. As the Bible is translated into various languages and brought into different cultural settings, idioms are taken into consideration. One spokesman from the American Bible Society reports:

We in the United States love the Lord with our 'heart,' but the Karre people of French Equatorial Africa love Him with their 'liver.' The Conob Indians of Guatemala love with their 'stomachs,' and the Marshall Islanders in the North Pacific with their 'throats.' But do all these different words in the various languages distort the message? Not at all. In each tongue they are synonymous with the overall sense of the original. Though we say, 'We press toward the goal' (Phil. 3:14), and the Navajo Indians say, 'I run with my mouth open,' it is one and the same truth.

We see that knowing the background, customs, and culture of the Bible will help us interpret and apply its true meaning to our lives. But how can we find out these things? First of all, we need to read the Bible regularly. The more we learn the Scriptures as a whole, the more we'll be able to understand some of these things. The Old Testament is background for the New Testament, and specific books provide background for others. For

69

example, the book of Leviticus will aid our understanding of the New Testament book of Hebrews. As a matter of fact, the author of Hebrews assumes his readers have a working knowledge of the Israelite sacrificial system. Much of the background for the letters of Paul can be found in the book of Acts which records his journeys and experiences in the cities of Philippi, Ephesus, Thessalonica, and others.

Studying maps is another way of getting the gist of the background. The maps in the back of the Bible are a good place to start, but atlases often provide more information and explanation. We can also look up cross-references that are in the margin of the Bible. Looking up the parallel verses will shed light on what we are reading. If we have some of the helps listed in chapter two, such as a Bible dictionary, we can look up certain words that will enrich our study. One final way to get a large dose of biblical background, though it may sound a bit expensive, is to go on a tour of Israel. It has been said that to visualize is to empathize. To travel to the land itself and see where all the events took place is worth more than a stack of books. Things that were once just ink and paper become a reality grasped by the senses. You will never read your Bible the same way again.

Principle #5: *What Does the Rest of Scripture Say?*

The term "balance" has become a modern evangelical watchword, and for a good reason. It's easy to get off balance—even among Christians. We can emphasize one doctrine to the neglect of all the others. We can use a "proof-text" to substantiate (albeit flimsily) almost anything in the world. We need the balance of the whole Bible for any particular interpretation. Our fifth principle takes this into consideration—interpret each passage of Scripture in light of the Bible's teaching as a whole. In other words, the *ultimate context* of any text is the *entire* Bible. One of the axioms developed in the Reformation still holds true: *Sola Scriptura Interpres.* Which simply means Scripture interprets Scripture. The importance of this can be readily understood if we read a section of Scripture and come up with an interpretation that contradicts the teaching of the Bible as a whole. At that point, we'd better put on the brakes. The Bible doesn't contradict itself. It has basically one author or superintendent—the Holy Spirit.

The Bible is a fabulous document. It is actually a compilation of many books with a unified message. Think of it, the Bible contains 66 books, written over a period of 16 hundred years by over 40 authors from different social backgrounds. The prophet Amos was a shepherd, Daniel was a political leader, and Joshua was a general. In the New Testament, Peter and John were fishermen, while Luke was a Gentile physician. Paul, the great missionary, was once a prominent Jewish

Rabbi. The Bible was written on the continents of Africa, Asia, and Europe in 3 different languages. It deals with controversial subjects such as the origin of the universe, the existence of God, and the purpose of life. One would expect a chaotic text with such variables and, yet, it reads as one unfolding plan of redemption. That's unity!

Imagine taking only 25 medical books from various cultures, written in different languages, over the last 1,000 years. Let's say we took folklore medicine of the American Indians and medical practices of Medieval Europe and then tried to treat someone based on all the findings. What do you think would happen to our patient? He'd probably be dead in a week! Yet, the Bible reads with synthesis and cohesion. It has successfully treated the sinful condition of man since its earliest days. That's why, when we interpret any particular passage, we must balance our findings with the rest of the Bible teaching.

In the previous sections we mentioned that most cults have gone astray because someone, usually its leader, took verses out of context. It's the same idea here. Much false doctrine has been perpetrated simply due to the notion that certain passages should be used while others are ignored. We can keep ourselves from such error by checking our understanding of a verse with the rest of the Bible. Don't isolate one section when forming a doctrinal position. For instance, if considering only Old Testament regulations pertaining to the Sabbath and dietary restrictions, without the balance of New Testament teaching, we might wind up as vegetable-eating Sabbatarians. The balance between the New Covenant and the Old Covenant, and the practices of the early church help to temper any unnecessary legalism. This is the reason one needs to read all the way through the Bible, and why a church needs to teach its congregation through the Bible. A little appetizer of the gospels and a midnight snack on the Psalms won't cut it. God gave it all and we need to read it all.

One simple way to consider this principle when studying is to look at parallel passages—those verses that discuss the same thing but are from another section of Scripture. Read, for instance, the miracle of the feeding of the 5,000 in all the gospel accounts. Details of the crucifixion are another example of how Scripture sheds light on Scripture. Each author wrote with a different purpose in mind. Seeing them back to back helps us get a fuller idea of what happened. If you're reading historical accounts in Samuel and Kings, find those places that parallel with the books of Chronicles.

All this talk of interpretation and critical thinking may sound a bit laborious, but just think of the payoff. You'll train your mind to muse over God's truths, extracting from them the utmost.

Like a child sucking an orange to get the last drop of juice, so let the life-giving nectar of God's Word seep into your soul.

It was M. A. Rosanoff, long associated with Thomas Edison, who had worked futilely for over a year to soften the wax of phonograph cylinders by altering their chemical constitution. The results were nothing short of negative. Rosanoff related how he mused night after night trying to "mentally cough up" every theoretical and practical solution. "Then it came like a flash of lightning. I could not shut waxes out of my mind, even in my sleep. Suddenly, through headache and daze, I was at my desk; and half an hour later I had a record in the softened wax cylinder.... This was the solution! I learned to think waxes...waxes...waxes, and the answer came without effort, although months of thought had gone into the mental mill."

Because Rosanoff thought "waxes," he came up with the answer. In the same way, when we meditate on God's Word, muse on it, analyze it, consider its context, language, background, and unity, its message becomes part of our very being. Direction and guidance will come from God when we think "Bible."

5

Open Your Senses

If you wish to know God, you must know His Word. If you wish to perceive His power, you must see how He works by His Word.
If you wish to know His purpose before it comes to pass, you can only discover it by His Word. —Author Unknown

Creativity is the gift of helping people see past the capabilities of their eyes and to see with their mind's eye. A creative communicator will be able to paint word pictures that help his readers or listeners retain critical information. The more vivid the picture, and the more senses the communicator can involve, the more lasting the retention. That's one of the great things about the Bible!

The Bible was not written in a format of systematic theology. Nor was it written in propositional theology, such as, "This is the doctrine of God including theistic arguments for His existence." If it was, most of us would use the Bible as a way to cure insomnia. But the Bible was written in a creative way by a creative God. He appeals to the senses of mankind so that His truth can be enjoyed and retained.

A lot of Scripture was written in story form. Stories reach out and touch our imagination and require our response as they draw us in and engender feelings. Stories do for us what lectures and seminars could never do—they touch us where we live. From the stories of David and of Ruth to the parables of Jesus, the Bible awakens our senses and involves our will. Just watch how a congregation responds when a pastor transitions his sermon with an illustration. It's like turning on a light inside—everyone perks up.

The Bible is also filled with poetry. As a matter of fact, there is an entire section of biblical literature known as the poetic books. They include the books of Job, Psalms, Proverbs, Ecclesiastes, The Song of Solomon, and the book of Lamentations. That's quite a chunk! These books portray the experiences of the wide range of people of God. Like most artists, poets live in a world of images. They think and speak without the restrictions of didactic communication. Figurative language comprises the colors of their literary palette. Their poems convey pictures to the mind's eye. So much of biblical literature is poetic that the use of images often intrudes into the prose of the Bible. Unless we can respond to this creative approach, we simply can't fully understand the Bible.

Let's consider the use of figurative language and its impact on our understanding and *enjoyment* of the

Bible. This chapter could be subtitled "Interpreting Figurative Language in the Bible 101." I hope you'll appreciate God's creative genius in making sure that His Book has the perfect blend of writing styles. (If this weren't the case, there would be more systematic theology sets sold than Bibles!)

You will find a glossary of terms in the back of this book for more in-depth study of biblical figures of speech.

Parables: Fiction that Conveys a Fact

Parables have been defined as earthy stories that convey heavenly truths. This definition stuck in my mind, as parables themselves are meant to. It's no secret that Jesus was extremely fond of using these stories when He taught crowds of spiritually hungry people. Storytelling was equivalent to ancient television. It engaged people's sense of imagination. A skilled rabbi could weave a story together in such a way so as to embed a truth permanently into the hearts of his audience. Perhaps that's why Jesus used them so much—He wasn't always dealing with people in a synagogue who were bound to remain until the end of the service. He often spoke to a crowd in the open air who were free to walk away at any time. Therefore, these stories peaked their interest and curiosity.

Parables are pretty easy to spot. Whenever Jesus used one, He always made it clear, as He preceded them by saying, "Hear a parable," or "The kingdom of God is like unto this...."

Teaching by means of parables is effective because it helps make abstract truth more concrete, interesting, memorable, and easier to apply to life. When a truth is externalized in the figures of a parable, internalizing the moral and spiritual meaning is easier and more powerful. Parables were not meant to give specific detail as much as to illustrate an underlying meaning that differed from the surface meaning. Some teachers pick parables apart and assign a figurative meaning to every detail. In doing so, the teller's original intent for the story is twisted. Parables generally focused on one teaching, one theme, and one point that Jesus wanted to get across.

We should be careful not to base or make doctrinal propositions from parables alone—unless Jesus Himself interpreted them in that way, and unless other Scripture can shed light on them for confirmation. In the parable of the sower and the seed in Matthew 13, Jesus explained the parable in great detail, giving us grounds for adequate interpretation. He explained that the field represented the world. He went on to say that the sower is the one who dispenses the gospel, and the seed is the Word of God. He named those points and details in the parable and then gave us their meaning. He taught us that Satan will rip-off people who close their hearts. A doctrine could be built on "the sower and the seed," because Jesus said it was that way. If He wanted to assign meaning to details of the parable, He told us their meaning; otherwise a parable has one meaning. We have no right to assume a meaning that is not plain in the text, nor to force a meaning just because we'd like to make it fit. That would be sloppy and irresponsible interpretation.

Typologies: Shadows of the Future

When you look at your shadow on a sunny afternoon, it's often elongated and distorted. It's not you, but it is an image of you. A shadow lacks substance but it resembles reality. In Scripture, we find this as well; there are shadowy types that depict spiritual truths. There are also "foreshadows" in the Old Testament of things to come in the New Testament. Listen to Paul's explanation in Colossians:

Therefore let no one judge you in food or in drink, or regarding a festival or a new moon or sabbaths, which are a shadow of things to come, but the substance is of Christ. (Col. 2:16, 17)

These feast days, or holy days, were merely shadows of future things. They formed a "prophetic shadow" or a prefigurement of the reality that was to be found in Jesus Christ. Consider the tabernacle of the Old Testament. We know what it looked like, we know how it was established, we know why God placed it in the midst of the children of Israel. However, the tabernacle was, in some respects, also a foreshadow of heaven. The writer of Hebrews, after explaining the ordinances of the Tabernacle, tells us about its typology:

But Christ came as High Priest of the good things to come, with the greater and more perfect tabernacle not made with hands, that is, not of this creation. Not with the blood of goats and calves, but with His own blood He entered the Most Holy Place once for all, having obtained eternal redemption. (Heb. 9:11, 12)

Continuing on a few verses later, he states:

Therefore it was necessary that the copies of the things in the heavens should be purified with these, but the heavenly things themselves with better sacrifices than these. For Christ has not entered the holy places made with hands, which are copies of the true, but into heaven itself, now to appear in the presence of God for us. (Heb. 9:23, 24)

The copies of the things in the heavens were but sketches, or outlines, of the realities of heaven itself. Christ did not go into an earthly Holy of Holies in the Temple of Jerusalem. He went into the presence of God—the heavenly, real Holy of Holies. With this in mind, it's fascinating to read John's account of his vision of heaven in Revelation. He sees the angels worshipping God, Jesus Christ, and the throne of God. We can readily observe how the heavenly realities follow the pattern of the tabernacle but then greatly exceed it in glory.

There are many types and shadows throughout Scripture, and they will delight any Christian who reads the Old Testament as well as the New Testament. The brass serpent in the wilderness was a type of Christ. How do we know? Jesus provided the interpretation Himself, "And as Moses lifted up the serpent in the wilderness, even so must the Son of Man be lifted up" (John 3:14). The Land of Canaan is a type of the victorious life we can have as Christians. The Sabbath represents a place of ceasing from our own works and resting in Christ. How do we know? Hebrews tells us in chapters 3 and 4 that these were models. Passover and the deliverance from Egypt are types of our deliverance from sin which is a constant theme throughout the Scripture. How do we know? Paul explained it to the Corinthians saying, "...For indeed Christ, our Passover, was sacrificed for us" (1 Cor. 5:7). Also, on the last evening before His crucifixion, Jesus took His disciples to an upper room and gave an old ritual new significance. He told them that when they took the Passover from that time forward, they were to do it with their memory fixed upon Him. Jesus was showing them that the Old Testament sacrifice of the lamb and application of its blood was a foreshadow of the sacrifice of Christ upon the cross. He was the Lamb of God who takes away the sins of the world.

A type is really a nonverbal prediction, an Old Testament person or event that illustrates some aspect of the person and work of the Lord Jesus Christ in the future but does not specifically describe it. You see that the writer has no way to see the future antitype. God's nonverbal predictions are as true and vivid as His verbal ones. However, a note of caution is to be sounded here. We cannot legitimately call a person or event a true Old Testament type except as the Bible itself reveals it to us. The only certain Old Testament types are those revealed as such in the New Testament. When the New Testament uses an example from the Old as a prefigurement of something that has occurred or will occur later, we can safely refer to the Old Testament example as a type. Ignoring such limits can quickly result in allegorizing and spiritualizing something without warrant. Because types are veiled revelations divine testimony to their identity must be given by the Holy Spirit in the New Testament.

Prophecy: A Window on Eternity

One of the most exciting and rewarding studies for any Christian is the study of prophecy. It's not hard to see that about one fourth of the Bible was prophetic when it was written. Once a pastor boasted that he did not preach on prophecy because, in his words, "Prophecy only distracts people from the present." His astute colleague skillfully retorted, "Well, then, there's certainly a lot of distraction in the Scriptures!" It's true. Much of the Bible includes a prophetic element.

Prophecy is history written in advance. It was Von Schlegal who noted that "A historian is a prophet in reverse." The prophets are God's mouthpieces about events before they exist. God, through prophecy, draws aside the veil of the future to give us an indication of what His plans are for the human race and the universe as a whole.

One of God's calling cards is fulfilled prophecy. He knows everything and predicts certain things before they happen and then they do happen! God said to Abraham, the patriarch, "Your descendants will be in a foreign land 400 years...." Guess what happened? They were! Through His prophets, God predicted the Babylonian Captivity even before Babylon existed as a military threat. He said it would last 70 years and guess what? It did! He further disclosed that Babylon would be overthrown by a character named Cyrus. The funny thing about it was that Cyrus wouldn't be born for another 200 years! Prophecy shows us that God controls history. Letting Him tell it is best:

> *"Remember the former things of old, For I am God, and there is no other; I am God, and there is none like Me, Declaring the end from the beginning, and from ancient times things that are not yet done, saying, 'My counsel shall stand, and I will do all My pleasure.'" (Isa. 46:9, 10)*

The study of prophecy is not a fruitless exercise. On the contrary, Scriptural prophecy, when properly interpreted, provides a guideline for godly living. It motivates Christians to the high standard of holiness. It's true that there have been those who have abused this sacred trust. Using the Bible, many have made erroneous claims about an event that turned out later to be bogus.

For instance, in 1870 a clergyman made a grave mistake. While visiting a small denominational college and staying at the home of its president, he expressed the firm conviction that the Bible predicted that nothing new could be invented. The educator disagreed. "Why, in 50 years I believe it may be possible for men to soar through the air like birds!" The visiting bishop was shocked. "Flight is strictly reserved for the angels," he replied, "and I beg you not to repeat your suggestion lest you be guilty of blasphemy!" Ironically, the bishop was none other than Milton Wright, the father of Orville and Wilbur. Thirty years later, near the small town of Kitty Hawk, North Carolina, his sons made the first flight in a heavier-than-air machine—the forerunner of the many planes that now dot our skies.

But we must not be deterred by those well-meaning-but-wrong interpreters who have misused the Bible. Prophecy is one of God's ways of revealing Himself to mankind, and these passages are some of the most important and fascinating portions of the Scriptures. God is not confined to space and time as we are, therefore, He can and has spoken of things to come. Prophecy is a powerful tool that opens a window on eternity. There are several types of prophecy that, when understood, allow us a clearer view through that window.

Some prophecy is fulfilled relatively quickly. In the deliverance of the children of Israel from Egypt, God said He was going to deliver them and did with a display of His sovereign power. The predictions about leaving their land of oppression would come to pass.

In the New Testament, Jesus often predicted His passion, death, and resurrection. This was not for some far off future time because just a few years later, He died on the cross. Sometimes prophets delivered contemporary messages that dealt with current problems and were not necessarily futuristic in their application.

Messianic Prophesies

I once read a newspaper story of an evaluation of all the prophecies made by mediums, horoscope writers, and other would-be prognosticators in 1986. They predicted everything from the economy to the presidency. Of the 600 predictions made, only 30 were actually fulfilled. Not a great record, huh? Predictions made by man are always replete with errors. But compare that with the 330 prophecies concerning Jesus Christ, given hundreds of years before His birth. All these predictions have been fulfilled concerning Jesus Christ's first coming.

Someone has attempted to calculate the odds of such events occurring (from a human perspective, of course) according to their predictions. It was estimated that the chance of these prophecies being fulfilled as they were written in the Bible was as remote as one chance in 884 plus 90 zeros!

Messianic prophesies are Old Testament promises that are fulfilled in the New Testament. They speak about Christ, His office, His person, and what He's going to do in the future. It is rather easy to see their fulfillment. Just watch for the way the New Testament authors make reference to Old Testament passages regarding Jesus.

Remember that prophecy was intended to encourage obedience. Even Jesus Himself warned His followers about the future so that they could learn how to live in the present. The idea wasn't so much that we would try and guess when they might be fulfilled but to help us remain spiritually alert and prepared as we wait for His return. Prophecy was also intended to give hope. News reports are typically filled with violence, scandal, and political haggling. They are depressing. But God's plan for the future provides hope and encouragement because we know He will intervene in history to conquer evil.

Unfulfilled Prophecy
In the Old and New Testaments

The Kingdom Age, The Millennium, and the Second Coming of Jesus Christ—when do these occur? When reading prophecy, especially in the Old Testament, keep in mind that we have an advantage the prophets lacked—perspective. We can look from the Old to the New Testament and see many prophetic fulfillments and understand how the plan comes together.

Think about looking at a mountain range from a great distance. The mountains would appear flat and one-dimensional, as though they were painted on cardboard and propped up from behind. However, if we got closer, or even flew over the mountains in an airplane, we could see the trees and rugged rocks, peaks and valleys. From this perspective, we would understand that the mountains are not flat at all but deeply layered. It's the same with prophecy. When the prophets of the Old Testament wrote, they saw two peaks without the valleys. They looked in the distance and saw the first peak as the coming of Christ and the second peak as the second coming of Christ. They often blended them together, not seeing a distinction from their vantage point. They didn't realize there would be a 2,000-year gap between the two events. They did not see the Church Age. Paul made this clear when he said the things of the church were not revealed in the Old Testament. This is called the "mystery of the church." We need to keep this concept of perspective in our minds as we look at prophecy, especially in the Old Testament.

There is a lot of debate these days concerning when Jesus will return. I hope it's soon and I believe it will be. Will it happen before the future time of tribulation that Jesus promised would come? I'm certain that it will. I know there is a lot of discussion about this, and there are as many views as there are people. Many are just plain bewildered by it all.

George Sweeting tells of a seminary student who was befuddled when his professor spoke about the pre-millennial view, the pre-tribulation rapture, the mid-trib, and the post-trib—until, finally, he was in despair.

He folded his arms, sat down, and said, "I.A.K."

And the professor said, "What does that mean?"

The student said, "That means 'I am confused.'"

The professor said, "Confused doesn't start with a 'K'."

The student replied, "You don't know how confused I am!"

I believe that the more we read God's Book, the more we'll see God's plan and realize that it doesn't include God's children going through the same judgment that the unbelieving world will experience. Rather than confusion, the study of prophecy will bring confidence and contentment in whatever comes our way by the will of God.

The biblical authors laced their writings with such vivid images that our senses are maximized. Through its stories, poetry, allegories, prophecies, and parables, we are able to have the truth fixed more permanently to the walls of our hearts. Let me close with a few hints on how to interpret these figurative expressions:

1. Interpret the text literally unless there's a good reason not to. Take the passage at face value unless there are other indications to do differently. For example, in Revelation 1:16 when the Lord appears, it says, "Out of His mouth came a sharp two-edged sword." I doubt this is literal. The interpretation would probably be figurative.

2. If the text gives you permission, then interpret it figuratively. For example, in Genesis 37, the dreams of Joseph are to be taken as prophetic because the passage says so. They are dreams that have a figurative application.

3. Figure it's figurative if it's a figure of speech. When you come across phrases like, "And He spoke a parable saying...." you know an earthly story with a heavenly meaning will follow. When you read words such as "like" or "as" you know that you're dealing with similes or metaphors.

Does all this Bible interpretation sound like a lot of work? Just remember the rewards that are awaiting you.

Think of the spiritual growth that is just around the corner. Think of the powerful tool you will become in the hand of God. Since this chapter was all about figurative language, allow me to close with a parable:

A man was out walking in the desert when a voice said to him, "Pick up some pebbles and put them in your pocket, and tomorrow you will be both sorry and glad." The man obeyed. He stooped down and picked up a handful of pebbles and put them in his pocket. The next morning he reached into his pocket and found diamonds and rubies and emeralds. And he was both glad and sorry. Glad that he had taken some—sorry that he hadn't taken more. Reach into the Bible and fill your heart with the jewels of God's Word.

6

Open Your Heart

Some Bible teaching is like swimming lessons on dry land. We have been taught all the things commanded by the Great Commission, but we do not observe them. Some know so much doctrine that an encyclopedia could not hold it, but what they know by experience could be put in a pocket notebook. We are afflicted with rocking chair religion and shade tree theology. We are like a man whose suitcase is covered with foreign hotel labels but who has never been out of his home state.—Vance Havner

On an average day, Christian bookstores sell 34,932 Bibles. But do they really make a difference in the world? In a village in the Fiji Islands, the Bible made a huge difference:

An agnostic college professor was visiting the Islands on business. After being in the village awhile, he remarked to an elderly chief, "You're a great leader, but it's a pity you've been taken in by foreign missionaries who only want to get rich through you. No one believes the Bible anymore. People are tired of the threadbare story of Christ dying on a cross for the sins of mankind."

The old chief, who was a believer himself, answered the professor, "See that great rock over there? We used to smash the heads of our victims on it. In that oven next to it, we roasted the bodies of our enemies. If it hadn't been for those good missionaries, the Bible, and the love of Jesus, we would still be cannibals, and you would probably be our supper."

I'm sure at that point the professor was thrilled that this tribe not only read but applied the Bible to their daily lives.

In the preceding chapters we have seen the importance of Bible study—how to observe and interpret. If we stop there, however, all our work has been in vain. It's the application of these truths of Scripture that makes the difference in our lives. It's where the rubber meets the road. Many times I'll hear a believer say, "I want to go somewhere where I get into the meat of the Word. I don't want this milk stuff." Whenever I hear that I'm inclined to remind them of what Jesus said, "My meat is to do the will of Him that sent Me," (John 4:34 KJV). That's where the meat of the Word is at—in doing what God wants. That's why observation and interpretation must always lead to application.

Jesus told a story of two builders, both of whom constructed nice homes. Though both looked great from the outside, one of these homes had a missing element—a foundation! Of all the places to scrimp, the foundation is certainly not the place. Then Jesus told the powerful story:

> *"Therefore whoever hears these sayings of Mine,*
> *and does them, I will liken him to a wise man who*

*built his house on the rock: and the rain descend-
ed, the floods came, and the winds blew and beat
on that house; and it did not fall, for it was
founded on the rock. Now everyone who hears
these sayings of Mine, and does not do them, will
be like a foolish man who built his house on the
sand: and the rain descended, the floods came,
and the winds blew and beat on that house; and
it fell. And great was its fall." (Matt. 7:24-27)*

In this passage, we immediately see the difference
between simply *studying* the Bible and *applying* what
we've learned in our daily living. It's easy to become
intoxicated by biblical knowledge and become reckless
and prideful. We must take the knowledge about God
and let it be transformed into knowledge of God. J.I.
Packer reminds us, "If we pursue theological knowledge
for its own sake, it is bound to go bad on us. It will make
us proud and conceited." We must guard our hearts
against such a prospect. We've all observed how wine
can cause an introverted person to become overly confi-
dent and say things he would normally be ashamed to
say. Empty biblical knowledge can have a similar effect,
puffing us up, leading us to try to impress others with
our knowledge of Scriptures. Without a personal commitment to love the people in our lives with His love and
live what the Lord has taught us, our spiritual talk will
sound phony and turn people away.

Some people become experts in the Scripture, yet their lives are unchanged. I once visited a friend of mine who had completed seminary. He could quote the theologians and give chapter and verse from the Bible, but after a couple of hours he looked at me sadly and said, "Skip, I don't think I know the Lord anymore." He explained that his seminary training placed a huge emphasis on head-knowledge but almost none on prayer, intercession, or pleasing and loving Jesus Christ. It was knowledge for knowledge's sake alone, and it led him to spiritual emptiness. He felt his study of the Bible had been just another discipline, like studying mathematics or science. What good does it do to have a full head and an empty heart?

The goal of studying the Bible is not interpretation but application. It's not just in finding a new tidbit of knowledge about prophecy or discovering the shade of meaning in a Greek word. The joy comes in finding the truth to apply to our own lives. It's then we can see that the Bible works! History tells us that when Crowfoot, the chief of the Blackfoot nation in southern Alberta, gave the Canadian Pacific Railway permission to lay track from Medicine Hat to Calgary, he was given a lifetime railroad pass in exchange for those rights. Reportedly, Crowfoot put the pass in a leather pouch and wore it around his neck for the rest of his life—but he never once availed himself of the rights and privileges it spelled out. What a tragic loss when Christians use the Bible as mere decoration, rather than turning it loose to work in their own lives.

Three Necessary Conditions of Heart

Application begins with our willingness to respond. We must be ready to react positively to the larger, encompassing principles of the Scripture. From there, we will be able to focus in on the transforming process of applying God's specific truths to our individual lives. There are a few prerequisites, however, for this to happen.

1. You Must Be His

The first, and most obvious step is that you must belong to Christ. A common complaint goes like this: "The Bible is too difficult for me to understand. When I read it, it doesn't make any sense." The problem may be that the heart is not changed. A person must be spiritually awakened before he can develop a spiritual appetite. Paul put it this way, "But the natural man does not receive the things of the Spirit of God, for they are foolishness to him; nor can he know them, because they are spiritually discerned" (I Cor. 2:14). First, make sure you have a personal relationship with God through Jesus Christ. If you are not sure, then right now admit that you are a sinner and ask God to forgive you. Receive Jesus as your Savior and Lord and then you're ready to start fresh.

2. You Must be Hungry

It was Jesus who said, "Blessed are those who hunger and thirst for righteousness, for they shall be filled" (Matt. 5:6). A spiritual appetite is a prerequisite to spiritual feeding. Peter would agree. He said, "...as newborn babes, desire the pure milk of the word, that you may grow thereby, if indeed you have tasted that the Lord is gracious" (I Pet. 2:2-3). If you are not hungry, you won't eat. If you are not aware of your need to seek God, you won't! In Hebrews, the Scripture says that God rewards those who diligently seek Him (Heb. 11:6). Look at Scripture like precious food to satisfy your longing soul. Ask God for a voracious appetite for His truths.

3. You Must Be Humble

Once you have an appetite for the Word, there must be a humble willingness to obey it. The best way to read the Bible is like an obedient servant waiting upon his master for instructions. The Bible is exciting when we apply its truth in obedience. God told Joshua:

"This Book of the Law shall not depart from your mouth, but you shall meditate in it day and night, that you may observe to do according to all that is written in it. For then you will make your way prosperous, and then you will have good success."
(Josh. 1:8)

Responding BOLDLY To God's Word

I read that Harvard astronomers have dialed outer space and are listening for an answer. Their ear, a receiving dish 85 feet in diameter, is located near Boston. According to a column in *USA Today*, this endeavor is the most extensive search ever conducted for intelligent life in outer space. The project is using a sophisticated, computerized radio receiver that allows the scientists to listen to and analyze 128,000 frequencies at once, 24 hours a day, for 4 years.

I wonder how many Christians listen to God's voice with as much determination and expectation. God speaks, but we must listen, and we must listen actively.

To help remember the process of making Scripture apply to your personal life, here's an acronym you can commit to memory:

Believe God's Statements of Truth
Obey His Commandments
Learn From Scriptural Examples
Declare God's Promises For Your Own

Believe God's Statements of Truth

In the Scriptures, there are blanket statements of truth that contain no promises, conditions, warnings, or challenges. When we encounter these statements, we are called to flatly believe what God has said. The Bible declares, for example, that God is love—no debate, no qualifying circumstances. We are to just believe this, as well as other biblical facts. This will help frame our understanding of the nature and character of God.

Sometimes blanket statements of truth will be attached to a promise or a condition. For instance, Jesus said, "God is Spirit." This statement of truth is followed by a condition: "God is Spirit, and those who worship Him must worship Him in spirit and truth" (John 4:24).

In Psalm 19, we find a blanket statement of the nature of God in regard to His sovereignty over creation:

The heavens declare the glory of God; and the firmament shows His handiwork. Day unto day utters speech, and night unto night reveals knowledge. There is no speech nor language where their voice is not heard. Their line has gone out through all the earth, and their words to the end of the world. (Ps. 19:1-4)

When we read this, our response needs to be, "I'm going to believe and stand on that as 100 percent fact, whether I feel it or see it, because it's in the Word." Some of the statements of Scripture may fly in the face of modern philosophy. Let them. You don't have to dance around them or be God's lawyer. Dwight Hall outlined this little piece to illustrate:

Some say: "Everyone is basically good."

God says: "All have sinned" (Romans 3:23).

Some say: "There is no hell, so there's no need to be concerned."

God says: "Fear him who...has power to throw you into hell" (Luke 12:5).

Some say: "Heaven is not a real place."
God says: "I go to prepare a place for you" (John 14:2).

Some say: "There is no such thing as life after death."
God Says: "Man is destined to die...and after that...judgment" (Hebrews 9:27).

Some say: "We can do nothing about the future. What is going to be will be."
God says: "You must be born again" (John 3:7). How can you be born again? "Whoever confesses and renounces [his sins] finds mercy" (Proverbs 28:13). "To all who received Him [Christ]...He gave the right to become children of God" (John 1:12).

Some say: "We cannot be sure of salvation or our destiny when we die."
God says: "You may know that you have eternal life" (I John 5:13).

Obey His Commands

Many times in the Bible God commands us to do something or to avoid doing something. Jesus said, for instance, that a man must be born again. He didn't say man should consider this option, He said we must be born again. If we fail to obey this command there are consequences. "Jesus answered and said to him, 'Most assuredly, I say to you, unless one is born again, he cannot see the kingdom of God'" (John 3:3).

Another example is the command that we repent of our sins, "The time is fulfilled, and the kingdom of God is at hand. Repent, and believe in the gospel" (Mark 1:15). Repentance is not an option, it's a commandment. I once heard someone say, "Oh Lord, forgive my hang-ups." Listen, God is not in the business of forgiving hang-ups, He forgives sins. We must be willing to recognize sin for what it is and obediently bring it before God in repentance. Even after we come to Christ, there will still be areas that require repentance.

There were times when God singled out an individual or a group in the Scripture and commanded them to do something specific. If there is no direct application to us, how do we regard these commands? Let's look at such a Scripture in Matthew 19:

Now behold, one came and said to Him, "Good Teacher, what good thing shall I do that I may have eternal life?" So He said to him, "Why do you call Me good? No one is good but One, that is, God. But if you want to enter into life, keep the commandments." He said to Him, "Which ones?" Jesus said, "'You shall not murder,' 'You shall not commit adultery,' 'You shall not steal,' 'You shall not bear false witness,' 'Honor your father and your mother,' and, 'You shall love your neighbor as yourself.'" The young man said to Him, "All these things I have kept from my youth. What do I still lack?" Jesus said to him, "If you want to be perfect, go, sell what you have and give to the poor, and you will have treasure in heaven; and come, follow Me." (Matt. 19:16-21)

In telling this young man to sell everything he had, Jesus gave specific instructions to a particular person in a certain condition. Because He knew his possessions were a hindrance to him, Jesus told him to sell what he had. His wealth was his god. From the context, and by the way the young man responded, we see how true this was, "But when the young man heard that saying, he went away sorrowful, for he had great possessions" (Matt. 19:22).

Money and possessions may not be a hindrance for us. We might even be broke, or perhaps we use our money to give to those in need. Although this command was to a specific individual, we find a timeless principle at the root of the command: *We must rid our lives of anything that hinders our relationship with God.* It may not be money. It may be a relationship with someone or a position of power on the corporate ladder. In going to the root of the commandment, we can find the principle and draw our own personal application.

Learn By Scriptural Examples

Living illustrations from the Bible allow us to see flesh and blood examples of both positive and negative behavior. When the Bible tells us about its heroes it doesn't hide the fact that they often floundered, fumbled, and made huge mistakes. Think of David's life for example. Before he repented he was an adulterer, a murderer, even a terrorist, yet God called him a man after His own heart. I take great hope in that! We see a tenderness in David that is rare even among God's people. In Psalm 27 we find a beautiful example of David's open heart before the Lord:

> *The Lord is my light and my salvation; whom shall I fear? The Lord is the strength of my life; of whom shall I be afraid? ...One thing I have desired of the Lord, that will I seek: That I may dwell in the house of the Lord all the days of my life, to behold the beauty of the Lord, and to inquire in His temple. (Ps. 27:1, 4)*

Continuing in this psalm, we see how responsive David was to the Lord:

> *When You said, "Seek My face," my heart said to You, "Your face, Lord, I will seek." ...When my father and my mother forsake me, then the Lord will take care of me. (Ps. 27:8,10)*

What an awesome example of love and trust in the Lord! Though David was a flawed vessel in many ways, he would return to prayer and worshipping God. We take his words as an example of the way we should present our hearts before the Lord. We learn from the example of God's people all throughout the Scripture. These are the "great cloud of witnesses" who have run the race before us (Heb. 12:1). We read of their lives, and because of their example we think, "If they can do it, by God's grace, so can I." Nothing could be more inspiring.

In Scripture we also find examples of what we should avoid. A striking example is in 1 Corinthians 10. Going back to the Old Testament times, Paul used the children of Israel as examples of what not to do. (They happened to fit that calling quite well). In fact, Paul underscored this when he told the Corinthian believers:

Now these things became our examples, to the intent that we should not lust after evil things as they also lusted. And do not become idolaters as were some of them. As it is written, "The people sat down to eat and drink, and rose up to play." Nor let us commit sexual immorality, as some of them did, and in one day twenty-three thousand fell; nor let us tempt Christ, as some of them also tempted, and were destroyed by serpents; nor murmur, as some of them also murmured, and were destroyed by the destroyer. Now all these things happened to them as examples, and they were written for our admonition, on whom the ends of the ages have come. (1 Cor. 10:6-11)

The message is clear. These guys are examples—bad examples. Learn from them and don't do what they did. As the old axiom goes, "Those who fail to learn from history are doomed to relive it!"

Declare God's Promises For Your Own

In 1956, *Time* magazine carried an article about a schoolteacher named Everett R. Storms of Kitchner, Canada, who, after his 27th reading of the Bible, decided to tally up all the promises in the Bible. This formidable task took about a year and a half. Storms came up with 7,487 promises that God made to man. So how are we to regard God's promises?

A popular creed these days is "find a promise and claim it!" However, there's more to claiming a promise than announcing, "I take that promise, amen." To claim a Scripture requires an open heart and a willingness to accept whatever God's will might bring in conjunction with the promise. Some of God's promises are assurances of blessing, while other promises are assurances of judgment and punishment. We must remember that even these *negative* promises carry just as much weight as the popular *positive* ones everybody loves to quote.

There are two kinds of promises: unconditional and conditional. An unconditional promise is when God said He will do something regardless of our actions. It is the declaration of a certain purpose of God which will be fulfilled in God's way and time. The covenant God made with Noah was an unconditional covenant with unconditional promises. It revealed God's purpose for the human race subsequent to Noah. Notice that God said He will accomplish it:

And God said: "This is the sign of the covenant which I make between Me and you, and every living creature that is with you, for perpetual generations: I set My rainbow in the cloud, and it shall be for the sign of the covenant between Me and the earth. It shall be, when I bring a cloud over the earth, that the rainbow shall be seen in the cloud; and I will remember My covenant which is between Me and you and every living creature of all flesh; the waters shall never again become a flood to destroy all flesh." (Gen. 9:12-15)

God made promises to Abraham that were unconditional. God said He would bring personal blessing to Abraham and make a great nation emerge through his descendants. Through Abraham, blessings would come to the whole world:

"I will make you a great nation; I will bless you and make your name great; and you shall be a blessing. I will bless those who bless you, and I will

curse him who curses you; and in you all the families of the earth shall be blessed." (Gen. 12:2, 3)

Supremely, this blessing would be fulfilled through Jesus Christ, who would be a descendant of Abraham. Abraham didn't have to do anything to experience these promises, God gave them with no strings attached.

On the other hand, a conditional promise consists of two parts: God's and ours. God promises to do something for us, if we do what He requires. Many promises in the Scripture are conditional. We have already looked at Philippians 4:19, "And my God shall supply all of your needs according to His riches in glory by Christ Jesus." The five verses before this one reveal the conditions of this promise. The Philippians had faithfully and sacrificially provided for Paul's needs. Because of their selfless care for him as He served God, they would experience God's care and provision for their own needs. Lifting that promise out of context distorts the message and intent.

An Old Testament example of a conditional promise is in Deuteronomy 28. God promised the nation blessings and fruitfulness, conditioned upon their obedience. But He also gave the other side of the coin—unfaithfulness and disobedience would negate the promises. In such cases, God's promises of blessings are contingent on the little word "if."

When we come across a promise in the Scripture that

has a condition, we have no right to jump in and lay claim to it unless we are obedient to the condition. We can't just underline part of it and say, "I claim it. I stand on it, in Jesus' name. It's mine, that settles it." We've got to be willing to meet the condition of human responsibility—obey the commandments and *then* claim the promises. To lay claim to God's promises we must step out and believe what He said.

William Penn, the founder of the commonwealth of Pennsylvania, was popular with the Indians. Once they told him he could have as much of their land as he could encompass on foot in a single day. So, early the next morning, he started out and he walked until late that night. When he went to claim his land the Indians were greatly surprised, for they really didn't think he would take them seriously. But they kept their promise and gave him a large area which today is part of the city of Philadelphia. William Penn simply believed what they said, and acted accordingly. How many promises of God are left untapped because we didn't believe them?

Transforming Your Quiet Times of Study

It's early morning and the house is quiet. You sit down with your Bible and your notebook, anxious to spend time with God in His Word. You are prepared. You have prayed for an attitude of receptivity and sacrificial devotion. You know the steps of observation and the process of interpretation. Now, you want to lift God's truths off the page and into your heart by applying them to your life. But how? Sometimes we understand something on an intellectual or conceptual level, but we get confused when it's time to act on our knowledge. The following guidelines for self-examination will take the edge off the mystery of applying God's Word. In the context of the passage you are studying, ask yourself:

1. How does this apply to my life?

How does the passage I just read apply to my job, my nation, my relationships, my neighbors, and my life *today?*

2. What changes must I make?

Now that this truth revealed to me, what changes must occur in my life? Is there something I must do or not do based on this text?

3. How will I carry out those changes?

How am I going to implement the changes based on this truth?

4. What will my personal prayer be concerning this truth?

What is my prayer going to be regarding the truth I just read?

5. What verse in this section should I memorize?

Which verse should I memorize that best summarizes this portion of Scripture? I chose: "Your word I have hidden in my heart, That I might not sin against You" (Psalm 119:11).

6. What illustration or word picture can I use?

In this vital phase of our study, we leave the role of the student and step into the role of the heart surgeon. We have only one patient, one whom we know very well, because the ailing heart is our own. We will examine our hearts under the revealing light of Scripture, searching for areas of sin and weakness. God is the Master-Surgeon directing the operation through His Holy Spirit. We will make a plan for correcting and strengthening those areas. We will hide God's Word in our hearts to keep us from future sin. And finally, we will lift up our concerns and repentance in prayer to the Great Physician for His healing, guiding touch.

Bringing It All Together: A Practice Session

Let's give it a try. In John chapter 4 we find the familiar story of Jesus and the woman at the well of Samaria. In this passage, let's briefly utilize some of the processes we've learned for studying and enjoying the Bible.

> *The woman said to Him, "Sir, I perceive that You are a prophet. Our fathers worshipped on this mountain, and you Jews say that in Jerusalem is the place where one ought to worship." Jesus said to her, "Woman, believe Me, the hour is coming when you will neither on this mountain, nor in Jerusalem, worship the Father. You worship what you do not know; we know what we wor-*

ship, for salvation is of the Jews. But the hour is coming, and now is, when the true worshippers will worship the Father in spirit and truth; for the Father is seeking such to worship Him. God is Spirit, and those who worship Him must worship in spirit and truth." (John 4:19-24)

As we begin the process of observation, we ask and answer the obvious questions as a journalist would: Who is involved in this passage? Jesus and a Samaritan woman. When did this take place? It took place when Jesus was in Samaria on His way to Jerusalem. Continue on with this process, asking questions of the text and writing down what you learn.

In verse 21 we gain insight as to the interpretation of this passage, "Jesus said to her, 'Woman, believe me, the hour is coming when you will neither on this mountain, nor in Jerusalem, worship the Father.'" Through observation and interpretation, and with the aid of study helps like a Bible dictionary, we learn that the Jews and Samaritans hated one another. After many bitter years of contention they had separate places of worship. The Jews worshipped sacrificially only in Jerusalem, while the Samaritans responded to this exile by building their own little rival temple on Mount Gerizim. The Samaritans were told if they really wanted to worship God the right way they should keep their worship at the temple on Mount Gerizim rather than going to

Jerusalem. The woman at the well had been brought up hearing that the Gerizim Temple was the only true church.

The Samaritans' claim was based on Moses' instructions to the Israelites concerning their entrance into the Promised Land. He commanded them to set up an altar on Mount Ebal and to divide the tribes: half on Ebal and half on Gerizim. The Jews held that since Solomon had been commissioned to build the temple in Jerusalem, the center of worship should be located there. The controversy was endless, and Jesus did not intend to allow Himself to be drawn into a futile discussion. Because of their hatred, the Jews would not touch a Samaritan. If they did, they were considered ceremonially defiled and had to go through ritual cleansing. Knowing this background, it's especially interesting that Jesus went out of His way to go to Samaria while traveling to Jerusalem. He deliberately went there for the purpose of speaking to this woman.

Now that we've gone through a quick process of observation and interpretation, we're ready for the next step of application. To illustrate this step, I'll share some of my own processes of application:

1. How does this truth apply to my life?

The first thing that strikes me in the passage is that it doesn't matter where I worship; as much as it matters *that* I worship the true and living God. I could be in an ornate church with stained glass windows, a storefront assembly, my home, my garage, or in my car. I could worship with a guitar, piano, organ, or with no music at all. The externals of worship don't matter. It's not the art of worship that is vital; it's the heart of worship that counts. Certainly, I must worship according to God's directives, but the important issue is that my heart is involved and that I'm not focused on outward appearances. There must be sincerity and truth. The truth I am applying to my life is that God wants me to worship in Spirit and in truth.

2. In light of this truth, what changes must I make?

I could concentrate my efforts on my personal devotional life. During my devotional time, I could search the Scriptures concerning worship and take my cues from them. I could determine that I will come to Him in my quiet times and begin each session with a concentrated time of worship. Intercession and personal requests will come afterwards. My first priority will be to bare my heart in praise and worship. Perhaps I'll recite a psalm or sing a song or even compose one that best expresses my heart of praise to God that day.

3. How will I carry out those changes?

Now, I will develop an active, practical plan to carry out these changes. In my study on worship, let's say I read a psalm that gives me further direction in worship:

Let us come before His presence with thanksgiving; let us shout joyfully to Him with psalms. For the Lord is the great God, and the great King above all gods...Oh come, let us worship and bow down; let us kneel before the Lord our Maker...Today, if you will hear His voice: "Do not harden your hearts...." (Ps. 95:2,3,6,8)

So now when I come before God, I'll thank Him for some specific blessings. In conjunction with John 4, I understand how to come into God's presence: to bow down and raise my hands. I know not to harden my heart, but to respond to His voice. When I gather with other believers in fellowship, I'm going to come prepared for worship. Why? Because the Father is seeking those who will worship in Spirit and in truth and I want to be one who does just that.

4. What will my prayer be concerning this truth?

Believing that God has spoken to me in His Word about this specific issue of worship, I want to be sure to respond to Him accordingly: "Lord, You are so worthy of praise. Forgive me for the lack of praise in my life and change that from today onward. Even as You are seeking those to worship You in spirit and truth, let me be found among those who please You in this manner. Help me not to be concerned with appearances or places, but help my heart to honestly express love to You."

5. Which verse(s) should I commit to memory that captures this truth?

I've picked verse 24 because, for me, it sums up the

meaning of this text. "God is Spirit, and those who worship Him must worship Him in spirit and truth." I can easily jot it down, keep it with me to memorize it, and make it the verse I meditate on for the day. (Imagine how much we would benefit if we did this 365 days a year?)

6. What mental image can I create that will help me share this truth with others?

I picture in my mind two mountains with a man kneeling in between them with his hands raised—and then I've crossed out the mountains. This reminds me that the external form of our worship is unimportant. Whether we are kneeling on a mountaintop or sitting in a sanctuary is of little significance. The important thing is to have a sincere heart as I worship God.

You're On Your Way

This approach can be used on a daily or weekly study basis. The more you do it, however, the richer the dividends. One anonymous author gives this description of the Bible:

This Book is the mind of God, the state of man, the way of salvation, the doom of sinners, and the happiness of believers. Its doctrines are holy, its precepts are binding; its histories are true, and its decisions are immutable. Read it to be wise, believe it to be safe, practice it to be holy. It contains light to direct you, food to support you, and comfort to cheer you. It is the traveler's map, the pilgrim's staff, the pilot's compass, the soldier's sword, and the Christian's character. Here paradise is restored, heaven opened, and the gates of hell disclosed. Christ is its grand subject, our good its design, and the glory of God its end. It should fill the memory, rule the heart, and guide the feet. Read it slowly, frequently, prayerfully. It is a mine of wealth, a paradise of glory, and a river of pleasure. Follow its precepts and it will lead you to Calvary, to the empty tomb, to a resurrected life in Christ; yes, to glory itself, for eternity.

Once you've practiced the principles of observation, interpretation, and application, they will be less mechanical and become second nature to you. Your time in the Word will be more rewarding, because you will be able to extract much more truth at each sitting. As you determine to live these truths, they will transform your life and Bible study will become, as Jeremiah put it, "the joy and the rejoicing" of your heart. There is no other book that compares. The Bible stands alone as the giant towering above all others.

7

Glossary

Anthropomorphisms

Words that attribute the physical likenesses or qualities of man to God.

Anthropopathisms

Words that attribute human emotions to God.

Concordance

An alphabetized index of Bible words.

Context

The explanatory words, ideas, and verses surrounding a particular statement in a discourse.

Dynamic Equivalent

A Bible version which sacrifices word and sentence structure for smooth reading and comprehension.

Exhaustive Concordance

An alphabetized index of every word in the Bible and a listing of all the passages in which it appears.

Expository Dictionary
A dictionary of biblical words that gives detailed and expanded definitions.

Figurative Language
A word, phrase, or expression used in a figurative rather than a literal sense.

Hebrew Parallelism
A style of poetry in which one thought is parallel to another, either supporting or contradicting it.

Hebrew Poetry
An ancient style of poetry in which the thoughts, rather than the words were rhymed.

Hyperbole
An exaggeration or an extravagant statement used as a figure of speech in order to emphasize a point.

Irony
An expression marked by a deliberate contrast between the apparent and intended meaning, leading the reader to see it as incredible or ridiculous.

Metaphor
A compressed or intensified version of the simile. Rather than saying something is "like" or "as" something else, as a simile does, the metaphor says one thing *is* another thing.

Metonymy
A word or idea that is substituted for something else. The replacement emphasizes perspective in a climactic way.

Parable
A story that teaches a truth or a lesson.

Personification
A figure of speech in which human qualities are attributed to inanimate objects.

Simile
A figure of speech in which two essentially unlike things are compared, often introduced by "like" or "as."

Typology
A prophetic symbol of something or someone to come.